HEALTH
is in the
SPIRIT

~∽~

WE ARE ALL WE NEED

CLAUDIA BURDICK

Health is in the Spirit

Library of Congress Control Number: 2009902634

Copyright © 2009 by Claudia Burdick

This book was written to empower people to explore different avenues of healing. It is not intended to replace medical advice or the services of your doctor. If you choose to use any of the techniques and information in this book, you are treating yourself. This is your constitutional right in the United States. You are responsible for choosing for yourself; we assume no responsibility for your choices.

No part of this book may be reproduced without the author's written consent.

ISBN: 1-4392-4486-3
ISBN13: 9781439244869

Dedication

This book is dedicated to all my children, and to my dearest granddaughter, Lily, who makes each moment a joy. With her innocence and acceptance, she has healed all our hearts.

Table of Contents:

Foreword... vii
Introduction.. xi
Section 1.. xvii
Respiratory System/Love 1
Lungs/Kindness 8
Cardiovascular System/Joy.......................... 10
Blood/Making Progress 17
Heart/Meaning 19
Endocrine System/Peace............................. 20
Thyroid/Certainty... 27
Adrenals/Sensibility (or Common Sense) 29
Pancreas/Loyalty 31
Excretory System/Patience......................... 33
Kidneys/Coherent and Consistent Assurance 38
Bladder/Uplifted 40
Nervous System/Gentleness 41
Brain/Justice 46
Skeletal System/Quality.............................. 48
Muscular System/Teachable 56
Digestive System/Temperance 61
Colon/Authenticity 67

Liver/Stability 68
Small Intestines/Highly Valued 69
Stomach/Strength... 71
Reproductive System/Faith 72
Uterus/Consciousness 79
Testes/Self-Esteem 80
Ovaries/Optimism 81
Prostate/Invigorated and Productive 82
Lymphatic System/Forgiveness 83
Integumentary System/Truth 93
Skin/Reliability 98
Immune System/Unity..................................... 99
Section 2...107
Quick Reference Guide to Systems, Organs, Glands 109
Quick Product Reference................................111
Healing Words...112
Gemstones, short and sweet 123
The Emotional Language of Essential Oils 125
The Essential Oil Profile List 128
The Essential Oil Nutrient List 143
The Essential Oils by Positive States 157
The Essential Oils vs. Negative States 165
Summary 172
Client Testimonials 175
Resources 182
List of Contributors and acknowledgements:..........184

Foreword

This book was written as a labor of love and passion. This is an incredible work about how energy from all of nature, spirit and man can come together to heal people of imbalances and dis-eases.

After many years of working with energies, life's twists and turns and tragedies, Claudia has been led to helping people find and heal the real cause of physical illness and problems. Through much searching, learning, and testing, she has brought forth a deeper understanding of why people develop illnesses and disease.

She combines herbs, the essences and aromas of flowers, gemstones, and energies of the universe together in various, unique combinations that match what the true vibrations of the different systems in the body need to operate optimally.

Everything in our universe, our world, and our bodies all have their own unique vibration and rhythm that enables them to function at optimal wellness and balance.

What we eat, drink, think, and do affects every cell in our body, along with everything else in the universe. Certain things will cause the vibration to shift, resulting, at times, negatively and making imbalances, dis-eases, and illnesses. This can occur before we are born or at any time in our lives. When this vibrational imbalance occurs, we can use nature to give us the nutrients we need to shift back into balance and health.

Claudia has put forth the beginning of a transformative type of healing that has great potential to heal our lives. She shows us that dis-ease and imbalances can come from a variety of factors, such as genetics, when we come into this world with issues, not listening or staying connected to God, our spirits, souls, emotions, bodies, or our lives. Claudia shows how working on these different levels with the nutrients that are combinations of nature's gifts such as gemstones, herbs, flower essences, aromatherapies, and energies, put together beautifully, are a key to a new and revolutionary healing system.

She has done much research and tested thoroughly to find this new and unique system using nature's bounty and goodness as nutrients on our bodies to enable the body to be brought back to wellness, wholeness, and balance on all levels. This book will show people that there is a new, transformative, gentle way to heal our bodies, minds, and souls from lives, events, and lessons that affect us. It will set you on a journey of healing yourself that is life changing.

Open your minds and hearts to a new and unique healing system that will enable your body, mind, and soul to reach their full potential.
Kathie Warpinski, N.D., Naperville, IL

Introduction

This book was born out of many years of working with my clients to find the solutions for the manifestation of their thoughts. For example, the manifestation of thought can appear in the physical body as a painful shoulder, a headache, or perhaps swollen ankles. What we have been focusing on, obsessing about, or worrying about does sooner or later appear in physical reality.

This can be good news or it can be bad news, depending on our thoughts and our willingness to accept responsibility for our thoughts.

It can also be old news as we recognize the pattern time and time again. Maybe we are the type that always seems to shoot ourselves in the foot. Just when things are getting good, we interrupt that good flow so we can follow our old pattern. We choose a type of partner over and over again that isn't healthy for us. We make the same mistakes in our career over and over again.

The newsflash is that the events in our lives are not random circumstantial events, but rather the unfolding and the embodiment of our thoughts.

The knowledge that all things possess a vibrational signature is not new information. We know that all things on earth, whether it be a gemstone, a plant, a tree, water, or flowers have their own unique vibration.

A vibration in layman's terms is the movement of energy within the object. The molecules in a substance are always moving and it is this movement that constitutes the vibration unique to that substance.

The signature vibration of each flower, each plant, each tree, and each gemstone is constant. There might be a little variation to their signature depending on the amount of sunlight or rain they receive or the condition of the soil they are planted in, but basically they continue to send out the same vibration or message year to year.

Daisies generally continue to have the same message whether they are a Gerber daisy or a field daisy. A daisy's message is peace and continues to be so throughout the whole daisy kingdom. A rose has a different message, but this message will basically be the same throughout the whole rose kingdom.

I began wondering why an herb such as evening primrose continues to benefit people for many, many years throughout history.

Why would the essential oil of peppermint help a person with a stomachache but also give relief for a pinched nerve?

Scientists would say it's the different chemicals within the plant that give these varied but consistent results. This leads us to understand that the chemicals in the plant are akin to a language. The plant contains these chemicals and when presented to the body, they are "interpreted" in the same ways in the body down through the ages.

So that would mean that there is communication between a plant and the body. There is a language between them that is understood. Now the question becomes, what is being said? What is the message of this whole plant? Why does the body continue to respond in the same way?

If you look in an herb book, you will see a whole list of mismatched symptoms and ailments that one little herb helps. For instance in *Indian Herbology of North America*, written by Alma R. Hutchens, evening primrose uses on page 123 are listed as: "to quiet nervous sensibility, this agent acts on alimentary toxins due to faulty diet and nervous tensions of long standing which create toxic waste, causing depression of the solar plexus and the central nervous system. Evening primrose stimulates the vital actions of the stomach, which has a direct association on the liver and spleen. Rendering renewed success in the treatment of gastro-intestinal disorders such as neuralgia, affection of the lungs, dyspepsia, hepatic torpor, heart, spasmodic asthma, cough of a nervous or spasmodic character, whooping cough, fullness of the bowels, and in female disorders associated with pelvic fullness."

What!?? But when we look at the message of evening primrose, which is "loving, let go, and mellow," we can see how it could affect all these different conditions. Now we can see how one plant does all that. Now we can see why evening primrose would help one person with a lung affection and another with fullness of the bowels. The answer of the "how" is in the message of the plant coupled with the present need existing in the body.

Setting out to discover the signatures of different substances was a very enjoyable and enlightening adventure. I started with essential oils since they were the most familiar to me. I was able to use the information gleaned from their vibrational signatures to help people see why they benefitted from a particular essential oil or herb. Taking this information to the next step, we used the vibrational signature messages to tell us what was going on in the conscious, subconscious, and even unconscious levels of thought. There were many "Aha!" moments when my clients began to see what was driving their behaviors.

As my clients and I worked with this new information, clear affiliations and connections began to emerge. This book describes these affiliations and connections—first we look at whole systems, then the organs and the glands within those systems, then their individual nutrients.

And speaking of nutrients, here is what we mean by this term. Nutrients are substances taken into the body that are then converted and used in a myriad of ways. Nutrients are usually thought of as proteins, carbohydrates, and fats. Nutrients feed the body, giving it the fuel it needs to complete its functions and processes. Our reference to nutrients is every bit as substantial as the food you eat. Love is a nutrient that feeds the body. Criticism and hate are poisons to the body. Even prisoners of war can subsist on very little actual food, but when they lose hope, their future can become tenuous. When we lose faith and fall into despair, ill health can and often does follow. When we are despairing and desperate, downtrodden and depressed, our well-being can take a dive.

Happiness is as beneficial to our health as the best food available. When our spirit is happy, our body is benefiting. It is in this vein of thinking that we present the various nutrients that feed the systems in the body. Truly health is in the spirit.

The suggestions for health enhancement given in this book are all non-intrusive and non-invasive. The flower essences can be taken internally or applied to the skin. Either way will work. You truly are in control of your own health by the thoughts you entertain and the contributions you accept from the world and others.

It is my joy to share this information with you, information that will empower you to take control of your happiness and well-being.

Claudia Burdick, author

Section 1

Respiratory System/Love

It's all around us: it sustains life for the entire planet. Without it, nothing would live. The air we breathe is free—it surrounds us and it is priceless. We cannot withhold this essential life-giving substance from anyone. It is everyone's birthright, whether we live in a mansion or a tent, in a prison or on free land, in New York or in China.

Air is abundant. Oxygen is an ever-present reminder that we are loved—each one of us, no exceptions.

Your water can be taken from you. Your food can be taken from you. Your privileges can be taken away from you, but your right to breathe cannot be violated. If your right to breathe is denied, your spirit will leave the earth in a matter of minutes. You can go without food for weeks; you can go without water for a few days. Without oxygen, you will die in minutes.

Air comes in through our lungs and is the catalyst for many wondrous processes. Our blood takes the air (oxygen) in our lungs to every part of our body. When we lose the ability to transport oxygen throughout our body, we lose some of our mental acuity. An oxygen-deprived body is an open door to disease: pain results in muscles starved for oxygen, strokes can occur when the brain does not receive enough oxygen. Every process in the body is dependent upon the oxygen brought in by our lungs and carried by our blood to every cell.

We all utilize love's beautiful components despite the fact that the concept of love is illusive. We can think of love as being appreciation, but "appreciation" doesn't come close to describing love. We can think in terms of sexual love, but that isn't "love" either. Even a parent's love doesn't completely describe love. What does love really mean? Many say that love is universal, unconditional, and freely given. If a person is deprived of love, he or she will wither. Give a person love, and he or she will blossom. "When you can't breathe, nothing else matters," says the American Lung Association. We could easily say when you can't love or be loved, nothing else matters.

When love is internalized, it manifests itself as characteristics that we recognize: respect, honor, appreciation, happiness, joy, a zest for living. These are the contributions of love. Oxygen taken into the body also declares its presence through multiple processes, whether those processes are being taken into the cells by the blood or out of them. It would be accurate to say that blood is not whole blood without oxygen.

> *"He who is filled with love is filled with God himself."* **Saint Augustine, 347.**

Love must also be present in other energy-creating productions to make them what they are; love is a part of all things. Without it, the structure and function of every part suffers—at the least, the parts are impaired, and at the worst, they shut down. This is reflected in society: those who live with love also live with happiness and peace. Those who are lacking love live a less-functional life. If you have love, it enriches every aspect of your existence.

The air we breathe comes from the stars and from the interaction of light with our atmosphere. The air is life's active ingredient—the continuous, interactive, enmeshed ingredient that we all recognize.

Oxygen is not something that some of us have and some of us don't. If we are living on earth, we all have oxygen coursing through our bodies. How do we obtain oxygen? We simply breathe. Even if we hold our breath and try not to breathe, we will pass out and automatically begin to breathe again.

Everything on earth has been infused with oxygen, whether it's the water you drink or the food you eat…or the tree you sit beneath. Everything on earth possesses oxygen.

Everything in your life also contains love. You might not recognize it at first, but it's there. The light that greets you in the morning contains love or oxygen. The water you drink has it too; so do the air you breathe and the food you eat. From that oxygen, other things come into existence. The elements that appear in your life show up because you create them from love. Love is the primary ingredient, which means that oxygen is a primary ingredient. It's the first ingredient—without it, nothing could exist.

Having enough oxygen makes everything easier. If we have enough oxygen, we can exercise more easily, run more easily, think more easily.

If we want more peace in our lives, we need to add more love. Peace will then be easier. If we want more joy, we need to add more love. Joy will then be easier. Use the power of your mind to see that love is everywhere and is freely available. Infuse it into your life creation. It has the power to change all perceptions, which in turn can change your reality.

Whatever your situation may be, think about adding love to it. See how that would change your situation. Is someone criticizing you? Add more love. Does someone hate you? Add more love. Is someone belittling you? Add more love. The choice is yours.

Love cannot be defined by anything, but by everything.

Here are a few suggestions you can easily utilize that point to messages of love:

Affirmations: Affirmations are little messages that we can incorporate into our daily thinking that help us move down the road toward fulfillment. You can write them out numerous times to plant them in your mind. You can sing them. You can meditate and pray with them. You can read them, but most important, you can ponder them as you go through your day and experiences seeing where you can change your thinking to serve you.

As you work with the affirmations you will begin to see little areas of thinking that are contrary to your happiness. Changing your thinking can change your life's savor and flavor.

Love is creative.
Love is ecstatic.
Love's true essence is unlimited.
Love touches all reality.
Love is benevolent action.

The Love Mandala. A mandala is a term taken from the Hindu language that means concentric energy circle. A circle represents protection, good luck, or completion. Mandalas link with the spiraling movement of consciousness and healing. This particular Love Mandala contains turquoise, amethyst, tourmaline, emerald, agates, and fluorite gemstones. These gemstones embody the certainty that all things are possible, that there is joy in going forward in life with compassion, and that love can be found in wisdom and simplicity.

The circular mandala represents eternal love. This mandala is available from www.burdickinstitute.com, or feel free to put these gemstones together and create one.

Metal can block the vibration of the gemstones, so you might want to use either silk, cotton, or Niobium wire to string them together. Niobium wire is the exception for using metal as this metal is a metal that has been used in the body in surgical applications and will not be rejected by the body. Niobium wire does not block the effects of the gemstones.

Sage Flower Essence is another practical tool to help bring more love into your being. Sage flower essences teaches whole-life balance, and integration of spiritual principles with practical applications for daily living. This essence helps us project our spiritual self through our personality self in our interactions with the world. It helps us be conscientious about the sounds we make, the words we choose, and the way we communicate with others; the essence guides us toward conscious choices of words and voice tones and toward speaking with kindness and gentleness. It offers spiritual inspiration and visionary guidance. It is useful in times of transition and life-cycle changes because it helps us redirect ourselves to higher life purposes and higher ways of living and being. (From *The Complete Book of Flower Essences: 48 Natural and Beautiful Ways to Heal Yourself and Your Life* by Rhonda Pallasdowney.)

Gentle Baby Young Living Essential Oil. Gentle Baby's vibrational messages are mercy, stability, relaxation, responsibility, and positive anticipation. It helps us overcome feelings of disrespect and inner pressures that stem from our need for outside approval. These messages aid us when we feel stifled and worried. (This essential oil is available from www.younglivingus.com.)

Love is the health-giving nutrient of the Respiratory System.

Lungs/Kindness

Oxygen exchange within the body has an impact on every system and part of the body; without oxygen, our bodies cannot live. As we learned in the previous chapter, Love is the nutrient of the Respiratory System. Love in the previous chapter was likened to oxygen in the sense that it oversees every function of our bodies and enhances every aspect of our life as it permeates our beings...

Likewise, kindness has an impact on almost all of our senses. When we see someone being kind, when we feel his or her kindness through a gentle touch or a welcoming handshake, or when we intuit the kindness of another toward ourselves or someone else, we can and often do experience an internal emotional response. It is through these senses of sight, taste, touch, hearing, smell, and intuition that we interpret our external reality. As these interpretations are brought inward our whole being responds to the information. Kindness can invoke powerful feelings and responses within us.

"This is my simple religion. There is no need for temples; no need for complicated philosophy. Our own brain, our own heart is our temple; the philosophy is kindness." **Dalai Lama**

When we notice the beautiful expression of kindness, it sometimes surprises us—because often, we had been expecting a different reaction. Kindness catches our attention because it's through kindness that we see and remember love. Just as life-giving oxygen is brought into the body through our lungs and then distributed throughout our bodies, love is given to us freely and distributed throughout our being by the avenue of kindness. The distribution of kindness occurs as we interpret the experiences life brings to us. Choosing to redistribute love through kindness enables us to breathe freely and enhance the performance of our whole being.

Cardiovascular System/Joy

What is Joy?

Joy is a nutrient that feeds the Cardiovascular System. Joy is unbridled happiness. Joy is the type of happiness that permeates every cell of our being. When we have joy, everything becomes possible. No task is too big; no burden is too great when joy is our companion.

In Ecclesiastics 5:18, Solomon said: *"What is the best thing to do in the short life that God has given us? I think we should enjoy eating, drinking, and working hard. This is what God intends for us to do. 19 Suppose you are very rich and able to enjoy everything you own. Then go ahead and enjoy working hard—this is God's gift to you. 20 God will keep you so happy that you won't have time to worry about each day."* (This quote is taken from the Contemporary English version of the Bible.)

Joy can keep us free from worry, from stress, and from caring too much about what other people think. When we are joyful, we can lay aside our cares about life. It isn't that we no longer have things that need our attention, but rather joy gives us the freedom to change our focus. Joy energizes us.

What is the cardiovascular or circulatory system in our body? The circulatory system consists of the heart, the blood vessels that are the veins and arteries, and the blood that circulates throughout the body. The blood absorbs nutrients from the food we eat and the air we breathe and delivers these nutrients to our cells. The blood also removes waste products. Blood is the one substance that we can find everywhere in our body. Blood is in our little fingers, our ear lobes, our organs, our eyes. And blood also carries oxygen.. Oxygen-deprived blood is unhealthy blood.

We know that we need joy, so how do we bring joy into our lives, and how do we engage joy and make it work for us? First, we must find our joy. Many of us have lost it; and others of us only possess a shadowy version of what we once had. We have tossed it aside, thrown it out along with the other things deemed unimportant. We have done this because of the ever-striving process of our lives—we've chosen to squeeze joy out of our lives because we believe we don't have time for joy and all the other things we want to crowd in. We don't realize that it is joy that makes our accomplishments worthwhile. Along with becoming constricted and hard, squeezing joy out of our days makes us poorly-equipped to roll with life's ups and downs.

If we have lost our joy, how do we cultivate or re-grow joy in our lives? We first have to find the seed. The seeds of joy are sown mostly in childhood as we play and discover what brings us joy. These little seeds of joy are still here—they're just waiting for us to replant them.

As a child, did you love to take walks through nature? Did you love to pick flowers? Did you love to sing just for the joy singing brought you? Or were you a child who exulted in the crisp crack of the bat against the ball, the mad dash for the next base, the roar of the crowd? Did you love to tinker with things, putting things together and taking them apart, designing better ways for Mom to get the dishes done, arranging things and implementing changes? Who you WERE as a child is who you still ARE.

To recapture joy, you need to revisit your childhood scenes of happiness. Even if you had an unhappy childhood, there were probably things you were able to do that brought you joy. Perhaps joy existed in your little collection of baseball cards…or your secret dreams of being able to go to a restaurant in the finest clothes you'd ever seen and order the biggest meal on the menu. Find the source of your joy and cultivate it.

If you can't figure out what brings you joy, then ask someone close to you when they have seen you joyful. Ask them to tell you what you were doing at the time–that might be a clue to finding your joy.

Now let's move on to how you can keep joy in your life and find more of it.

You keep joy by feeding it and nurturing it. You'll want to safeguard your joy. If your joy is in nature, for instance, you can bring more of it into your life by getting your hands in the dirt and planting some seeds. You can water your little plants and then enjoy watching them grow. You could collect some stones and arrange them in your house. You can give life to those beautiful scenes in your imagination.

If you were the child who delighted in expressing your physical ability and strength, then get out there again! Get off the couch and join a team—any kind of team. Your body might not let you run for the bases, but you still have the ability to hand out soup bowls to the needy, to stock the shelves at your local food bank, to be a part of a team. If you loved to tinker as a child, you might find your joy in restoration of a car, in the making of quilts, in designing a more efficient house, or inventing a more efficient, time-saving appliance.

We all want to have joy in our lives, but oftentimes we're too depressed to do anything about it. Perhaps we've already given up and given in. This is where the tools for joy come in, because there are plants and gemstones and flowers that have the essence of joy in them. Since they were created with joy, they continually emanate it. The following is a list of things that express joy.

> "Man is made by his belief. As he believes, so he is." **Bhagavad-Gita**

Yellow. You can wear yellow and absorb its vibration. You could paint a wall yellow. Put a yellow-checkered tablecloth on your table. Get a bright bouquet of yellow flowers. Use some yellow candles to decorate. Paint a picture using different shades of yellow—wild and with abandon—splashing yellows to match your joy. Hang up your picture and remember the joy you had creating it.

"It is the color closest to light. In its utmost purity it always implies the nature of brightness and has a cheerful, serene, gently stimulating character. Hence, experience teaches us that yellow makes a thoroughly warm and comforting impression. With yellow the eye rejoices, the heart expands, the spirit is cheered and we immediately feel warmed. Many people feel an inclination to laugh when looking through a yellow glass." Johann von Goethe. *Theory of Colors,* 1840

Sugar. Now just so you know, I am not advocating that you consume large amounts of sugar, but the actual craving for sugar tells you that you need to add some joy to your life. If you find yourself craving sugar, think of a healthier way to bring in joy. Feeling desperate for sugar should be an alarm bell to you that you need more joy in your life. Instead of caving into the craving for sugar, use some of these other tools to fill that void.

Amethyst gemstones emanate joy. Put them in your pockets; line them up along the side of your bed. Metal can block or deaden the vibration coming from all gemstones, so always try to use gemstones in their natural state. If you do desire to wear them and want to string them together for a necklace or bracelet, use leather, silk, or cotton cording so the vibration of the amethysts will be able to flow into your body. You can also use Niobium wire, which will not interfere with the body's vibrational fields. See the chapter on love for more about Niobium.

Flowers. Although many flowers possess the vibration of joy, sunflowers, daffodils, roses, lilies, and tulips are especially joyful. Living flowers, of course, have stronger vibrations than ones that have been dried.

Joy Triz. This triz is a beautiful creation compiled from the vibrations of joy. It contains the herbs of rose hips, rose petals, and turmeric, the essential oils of Joy, and rose and the gemstones of amethyst and opal. These ingredients are strong with the vibration of joy. These are encased in a geometric cube shape representing completion. A triz is wonderful to have beside your bed—you'll take in vibrations while you sleep—or anywhere you spend much of your time, such as in your kitchen or by your computer. The Joy Triz is a kiss of joy from nature.

Joy Savory. Savories relate to the sense of taste in the etheric, unconscious level of the body. The etheric body equates taste with hope. The Joy Savory is formulated to address the need for joy, especially the joy that hope brings. Joy Savories contain sycamore flower essence and tourmaline gemstones. Sycamore flower essence is from the Findhorn Flower Essences in Scotland; its key note is revitalization.

Sycamore recharges and uplifts body and soul when we are stressed or worn down. It helps us to tap into the unlimited energy source of the life force, the universal force that radiates, illuminates, and energizes our whole beings. Sycamore allows us to experience the smooth flow of energies in ourselves, in our lives, and in nature. Tourmaline speaks to us of eagerly looking forward. When combined Syacamore and Tourmaline will create a vibration of joy through hope. We call this combination Joy Savory.

Joy Tactiles. Tactiles are formulated to address the sense of touch, which is likened to forgiveness in the etheric body. They are meant to be waved or wafted through the auric field applying touch to the auric field. The Joy Tactile has chia seeds and garnets on the tactile wand. Chia seeds are known for providing stamina to the individual who is consuming them. Long ago, the North American Indians used them for strength during their long-distance runs. Garnets speak to the body of honor. The honor and strength that forgiveness brings to the body creates joy in return. Available from www.burdickinstitute.com or feel free to create one for yourself.

Joy is the health-giving nutrient of the Cardiovascular System.

Blood/Making Progress

The opposite of making progress is a standstill, a stoppage. The low-energy side of making progress is stagnation: slow movement and stops and starts. We all know that normal progress happens when we have a smooth start and calmly continue to move forward. There is a negative, high-energy side to making progress, however, and that's feeling frustrated and anxious—even angry—in the face of crunching deadlines. We tend to ignore our needs and priorities as we push ever onward.

Calm progression requires a knowledge of where we're going, what goals we have in mind, and a certainty that we will achieve our objectives.

"Purpose is what gives life a meaning."
Charles H. Perkhurst

When we don't know where we are going and we're not able to set goals, we move very slowly.

If we have a target in mind but are so single-minded that we ignore and/or push aside issues that are vital to us, we experience anxiety-ridden progression. Often, we proceed this way because we feel that we will miss out on something or be punished if we do not perform to high expectations. This type of progression is driven by a skewed perception of our self-esteem and self-value.

Heart/Meaning

Meaning is what gets us going in the morning and gives us peace at night. It is that deep inner value we give to our lives that provides sense and sanity in our world. It's our intrinsic life value.

When we lose our meaning in life, we start to flounder. Like a fish flopped up onshore we become unable to breathe, a feeling of the world closing in and suffocating us, and when this continues we become unable to make progress in life. When we lose meaning, and can't find our purpose, we can lose our desire to even continue living. We wonder why we can't make sense of the world anymore. Losing meaning results in a painful wailing inside of ourselves, a search for what we have lost and the anguish of not finding it. To lose meaning is to lose hope.

Having meaning is a delight, a guidepost, a compass that gives us our bearings in life. Having meaning makes our world upright again, even when things are topsy-turvy.

Endocrine System/Peace

Peace is not ignorant bliss. Rather, peace is an awareness that responds appropriately.

Imagine that you need information from your boss to meet an upcoming deadline. You keep reminding her that the deadline is approaching, but she doesn't answer. As the deadline gets closer, your peace doesn't increase—it decreases. When the deadline arrives, all is in turmoil.

This scenario represents an endocrine system going out of balance. Such imbalance occurs when our awareness does not or cannot respond appropriately. Maybe you are aware of things that you need to work on and change. Maybe you aren't aware of them…or you're choosing not to notice. You just keep putting off what needs to be changed, planning on getting to it someday. Time passes. The bliss-filled moments you have been allowing yourself warp into a crisis.

Your adrenals can no longer deal with receiving poor information, too much information, or erroneous information, so they begin to wilt under the stress. When you wake up the next morning, you look at your face and gasp in horror—the skin around your eyes is puffy and red, like pink tapioca. There's a pain in your back, and it's relentless.

Now you understand that those things you didn't want to face—those changes you've been putting off—are literally in your face and can no longer be ignored.

The endocrine system consists of various glands, such as the thyroid, adrenals, pituitary, pineal, and others. Sometimes it's hard to say which glands are parts of the endocrine system, which belong to the immune system, and which are part of the reproductive system.

We do know, though, that the glands produce hormones. These hormones are the body's informants. They run around the body, telling it what's happening and what the program is for the day. They might announce to the body that a lot of stress is about to come in—for example, if you're worrying about an upcoming presentation and don't feel prepared. Truckloads of worry will be delivered, and it's the duty of the endocrine system to deal with this cargo. The body will have to find a way to adapt.

Or perhaps you've prepared for this presentation and have done all you can for the moment. You respond by shutting down the faucet of worry because you know that when the time comes you'll do the best you can, so you tune in to another channel. That channel flips to a memory of a scene where your daughter is hugging your elderly mother…or maybe to the last time you went for a pleasant walk. You hear the crackle of the leaves under your feet, you smell the pines, and you hear the rushing of the waterfall just ahead. Your endocrine system responds in kind and makes you feel at peace and in harmony with your surroundings.

Most of us have experienced the above scenario, and most of us have probably turned our faucet of worry into a gusher. Time and time again, we pick up the luggage we've already kept for too long and continue to drag it along, even when we don't want it there.

It's interesting to note that WE (that's we, ourselves, and us) control the messages we give our endocrine system. The information we provide can be composed of stress and anxiety…or of grace and acceptance.

If the information is one of stress and anxiety, the endocrine system will respond in a negative way. When we see the results of this kind of information written in the strain around our eyes and in our body's aches and complaints, we'll look back and wish we would have changed our message.

If the information we provide is full of grace and acceptance, the endocrine system will respond in a positive way, with health and harmony.

Going back to the concept of the trucks coming into the warehouse, we can see that the response to the cargo in the trucks will depend upon the content of the cargo. If it's a load of fish, there will be provisions for that: refrigerated storage and temperature control. If the cargo is a pallet of lumber, humidity and temperature will have to be controlled.

Peace will reside in the warehouse when provisions have been made to accept and handle the freight.

The endocrine system is also constantly accepting the loads of information we send it. Minute by minute, hour by hour, it adjusts our hormones to reflect the cargo. We decide what the truck arriving at the dock will contain.

Peace is not ignorant bliss. Peace is an awareness that responds appropriately.

If we choose to be unaware of the cargo—i.e., our surroundings—the loads will continue to come into the dock without any controls in place. But if we choose awareness, we can minimize the damage caused by the cargo and can have productive and cheerful informants or hormones carrying valuable information to every part of the body, soul, and spirit.

How do we obtain this peace, this awareness? To relate this goal to the warehouse scenario, if something does come in for which the warehouse isn't prepared, whoever is in charge will have to make some decisions. Should the cargo be unloaded or sent on? Should it be distributed immediately or kept in storage? Maybe trucks from another facility will be arriving and expecting to use the warehouse. The overseer can decide to allow the trucks to unload their cargo anyway and cause utter havoc...or the trucks can be redirected to their appropriate destination.

How many times have we decided to panic because something unforeseen has happened in our lives? How many times have we felt that we just can't adapt? How many times have we allowed others to unload their cargo when there is no room or provision for that load in our warehouse? The good news is you're the person in charge. And the bad news is? You're the person in charge.

Your decisions affect every part of your being. *"The mere possession of a vision is not the same as living it, nor can we encourage others with it if we do not, ourselves, understand and follow its truths. The pattern of the Great Spirit is over us all, but if we follow our own spirits from within, our pattern becomes clearer. For centuries, others have sought their visions. They prepare themselves, so that if the Creator desires them to know their life's purpose, then a vision would be revealed. To be blessed with visions is not enough...we must live them!"* High Eagle

We obtain peace by choosing to be aware and to be responsible for WHAT we allow and HOW we allow it.

The following are some tools to help us become aware and conscious. With these tools, we can begin to take control of our own beings and create happy hormones that will result in appropriate responses within our bodies.

The Peace Mandala contains aquamarine, agate, fluorite, turquoise, tourmaline, onyx, citrine, sapphire, and opal. The many gemstones in this medallion provide the body with a well-rounded response for many situations. The Peace Mandala contains many messages: be merciful, use wisdom and simplicity, believe that there are solutions to every problem, look forward, be skillful, embrace the truth, and feel powerful and strong. If an organization were to instill these qualities in their employees, they would have a smooth-running company. The circular mandala represents the timeless circle of eternity. Feel free to create one, or it is available from *www.burdickinstitute.com*.

The Sun Planetary Tuning Fork. This tuning fork is tuned to the vibrational frequency of 126.22 (this frequency is believed to contain the frequency of the sun, corresponding to the color of yellow-green, affecting the Manipura, or Hara, (navel and 3rd lumbar vertebrae). It is said it enhances our senses of strength and motivation, self-identity, vitality, and radiance. It stimulates enthusiasm, generosity, creativity, assertiveness, and determination. The Sun Planetary Tuning Fork also opens the heart and enhances self-awareness, self-expression, and self-confidence. It helps us understand self-will and assists us in finding our purpose. The Sun Planetary Tuning Fork is available from *www.luminanti.com*.

Peace Wisdom Sachets. The sachets are combinations of herbs and essential oils. The Peace Wisdom Sachet contains corn silk herb, cyperus herb, bee propolis, black cohash herb, hyssop herb, asparagus root, chia seeds, and chestnut leaf. It also contains harmony, lavender, myrtle, frankincense, and clove essential oils from Young Living Essential Oils. Together, these create the vibration of peace.

Peace Wisdom Sachets are meant to be carried in your pocket during the day and throughout the night if necessary. Carrying the wisdom sachets are much like a rejuvenating walk through the forest; they provide your body with much-needed wisdom and peace. They work on an unconscious level of your being to impart vibrational healing to your endocrine system. Feel free to combine these herbs and essential oils yourself. (Wisdom sachets are also available from *www.burdickinstitute.com*.)

"Ruby Gem Elixir cleanses, balances, and energizes the first chakra and opens the lower chakras to a stronger flow of life force energy from the earth. The elixir supports your ability to ground spiritual and mental energy in the physical body, particularly during times of intense transformation." Taken from *A Guide to the Alaskan Essences: the Essence of Healing (Second Edition)* by Steve Johnson. (Also available from *www.alaskanessences.com*.)

Peace is the health-giving nutrient of the Endocrine System.

Thyroid/Certainty

The nutrient for the thyroid is certainty. In this fast-paced world of unexpected change, how can we be certain of anything? Even though it's true that there is much changing around us, there are things of which we can be certain.

We know the sun will come up in the morning. We know that night follows day. We know that no matter whether we live or die, our spirits and energies will live on. Okay, we agree on that, but so far that doesn't feel like much comfort. Let's go on.

We know that we are loved. We know that we are important. We know that we matter. We know that our lives have purpose. Ahhh………Now we can feel certain of that.

No matter whether we have trials and problems in our lives or whether our lives contain prosperity or pain, these are the things of which we can be certain. Whether we are joyous or sad, these things we can be certain of. We can be certain and know that our life matters—that everyone's life matters—this is the certainty that feeds the thyroid.

The thyroid is involved in digestion and in hormone production. Along with the adrenals, it is a co-regulator of the heart. The thyroid has a say in our weight, whether it's a gain or a loss. It regulates our body's temperature control.

Since certainty is a nutrient of the thyroid, it follows that fear depletes certainty. Fear causes panic. Fear causes withdrawal and hiding. When we are feeding ourselves uncertainty or fear, we are stressing our thyroid. Byron Katie teaches us that if a thought is not serving us but rather is distressing us and causing us anxiety and pain, we can just drop that thought. How would we feel without it?

I highly recommend Byron Katie's books, especially *Loving What Is*. You can find her online at *www.thework.com*.

Adrenals/Sensibility (or Common Sense)

Have you ever noticed that the people who experience adrenal burnout are the people who are very dependable and logical? They seem to possess an ability to stay calm during the worst storms of life. But when they crash, they crash hard.

Remaining in a constant state of hyper-vigilance can burn through our adrenal reserves of chemicals and hormones that keep us healthy. When our reserves are depleted we can experience swollen skin around the eyes, rashes, issues with our nervous system, and panic attacks.

Our adrenal glands are the glands that send out epinephrine. Epinephrine is an antidote to an allergy reaction. Sensitive people bring little kits with them when they go camping or hiking that contain epinephrine in case they come across an allergen they can't handle. Many times, this can mean the difference between life and death. Allergies cause our body to over-react. This over-reaction really stresses our adrenal glands as they try to compensate and balance. *Allergies come into play when our body misinterprets a substance as being harmful to us.*

When a substance really is harmful and not just a perceived threat by the body, we would call this a toxic reaction, or poison. Since all substances have a vibratory informational message, our body "reads" these substances and then reacts. An appropriate response to a poison is to vomit and sweat, which helps eliminate the poison from the body. Our heart will begin to race as it works to dispel the toxin. This is what we want our body to do! If you have allergies, though, you know that this is also how an acute allergic reaction feels. You've all heard of a person who is just allergic to everything or maybe you are that person. If so, take heart.

There is a book called *Cure Your Own Allergies in Minutes* by Dr. Jimmy Scott, the founder of Health Kinesiology, that gives a method whereby a person can re-educate the body as to what an actual threat is—poisons, chemicals, etc.—and what are merely perceived threats. With this method you can gradually experience a more normalized state of being.

Pancreas/Loyalty

That's you standing beside yourself.

This is a loyalty that believes in yourself to the point that you'll stand with yourself and by yourself if need be.

You will stand with yourself even when others think you're a little crazy or that you'll never amount to anything.

You stand with yourself even though you've fallen and have had to get up time and time again.

Standing with yourself means being there for yourself, standing by yourself with great conviction in your own worth and your own abilities...whether those convictions are understood by others or not.

This nutrient is a loyalty that is unconquerable.

When we cannot or do not feel loyalty toward ourselves, an unshakeable loyalty, the sweetness and joy of life can become distorted. How can we feel joy, real joy, when we do not value ourselves?

Giving up on ourselves, however disguised this may be, can cause deficit and dysfunction in the body resulting in problems for many of the body's systems, including but not limited to the cardiovascular system, the excretory system, and the digestive system.

Excretory System/Patience

Just wait. Have patience. Slow down. Does having to wait make you feel like grinding your teeth and clenching your fists and screaming, even though you check those feelings? We live in a very impatient society. Remember the Visa commercial, in which using slower-than-credit cash stops the whole procession of life?

In America, we live in a fast-paced society that prevents us from being able to observe and notice what is going on in our lives. Have you ever noticed that when you have to go to the bathroom, if you get busy, you forget that you had to go? (Although it's also true that, after a while, you'll be forced to go since you CAN'T wait any longer.)

When we take in nourishment, it undergoes a long journey to reach the kidneys and bladder, where it is voided. Our bodies take the nutrients out of the food and then get rid of the waste we can't use via the excretory system. The body has to work hard at extracting every little bit of nourishment from the food before it's expelled. If it were rushed through the body, *nutrients crucial for sustaining life would be lost.* This is why we are admonished to stop and smell the roses.

Patience means calmly enduring and patiently waiting. The kidneys don't shout "Hurry up!" at the liver. Instead, the kidneys wait patiently to extract and filter what the body needs and doesn't need. If we speed up the process of life so that we can just get through it, we will miss important, nourishing elements of life.

The kidneys produce renin, an enzyme, to regulate blood pressure. According to *Taber's Cyclopedic Medical Dictionary*, renin "is an enzyme produced by the kidney that acts on angiotension to form antiotensin I, a pressor substance. In some forms of hypertension, renin is elevated."

Sometimes the problem with high blood pressure lies not in the heart or the arteries. Rather, it's a kidney issue. Often, a problem with high blood pressure or anger or stress is not due to a lack of joy or a lack of meaning, but rather to a lack of patience. There is nothing like being delayed to get our dander up—we really hate that. It's infuriating.

Anger and impatience go together hand-in-hand— the ability to wait without anger is a rare sight. We don't often have the experience of calmly waiting without feeling anger creeping in. We feel it coming and persuade ourselves to turn it away, but then it rises up again. "Sheesh, where are they?" we think. "What time is it?"

Waiting patiently and without anger is accomplished through trust. The kidneys wait patiently for the other organs and glands to do their jobs so that it can do its job. When we have kidney and bladder problems, we might want to take a look at our issues with patience and trust. The idea of patience being a nutrient for the excretory system is a little hard to grasp because we aren't used to seeing patience as a virtue or nourishment.

Sometimes patience is even perceived as a weakness. But patience is born out of great strength. Some issues with the bladder and kidneys manifest themselves fully as an inability to wait and have patience any longer. The mechanisms that hold back the flow just cease working—we just can't hold it back anymore. The reservoir of patience has been depleted.

Sometimes it's just a little leak of impatience. As the leak progresses and we are still rushing and pushing, a day comes when all resistance is now gone. There is no control. We try to control and do as we have always done, but there is no response to our insistence. There are many problems associated with the kidneys and bladder, and if we have them, we cannot ignore them—we are reminded of their presence every day.

If we are out of patience, how do we replenish our supply? These are some tools that work on different levels of consciousness to help bring patience back into our life. Trust, peace, and patience go hand in hand, so try some of these tools and see what kind of difference they can make for you.

Affirmations: Speak them out loud, write them, read them, sing them, or pray them. Let the words sink down into your unconscious mind. Use them repetitively until you can live them. Our words are at the highest level of vibration that we possess. They are powerful and one of our greatest tools. Let them work for you.

Life uses comfort to instruct me.
I choose to be generous and loving and to build others up.
I have the power to create a wonderful life through patience.
I welcome instruction; I surrender to transformation.
Living is wonderful.

Aura-Soma Equilibrium (B25 Florence Nightingale). The product literature from Aura Soma has this to say: "A mystic, a pioneer who receives inspiration from above relating to the greater good. Letting go of disappointment and putting our caring into practical activity." This equilibrium is available from an Aura Soma practitioner.

Sleep is another aid that replenishes our patience. It allows us to let go of the expectations we have been "holding" so that we can relax and allow life to flow again. Be sure to get enough sleep—allow yourself naps, too, to restore your patience.

The Patience Mandala contains bloodstone, tanzanite, rhodochrosite, and topaz arranged in a circle to represent timelessness. Bloodstone gives us frequent refreshment while tanzanite guides us toward being resolute and settled. Rhodochrosite speaks to us of concentration and focus; topaz allows us to get out of a rut and grow. The

EXCRETORY SYSTEM/PATIENCE

Patience Mandala's message is: I am refreshed, resolute, settled, concentrated, focused, and growing. (Feel free to create this Patience Mandala for yourself or order one from *www.burdickinstitute.com*.)

> *Patience is the health-giving nutrient of the Excretory System.*

Kidneys/Coherent and Consistent Assurance

The kidneys filter liquid waste from our digestive system. When the kidneys don't function properly, fluid can back up in our tissues. This fluid retention is often apparent in the legs, feet, and hands. The kidneys are amazing—they do more than just filter liquid waste. They also are involved in hormone production and many other processes. Understanding the kidneys and their functions requires many years of exacting study and preparation.

When we're certain of something, we can relax. When we feel assured, we can skip worrying and let go. Assurance is not just being certain, however. It's a little step beyond that, a step that takes us to a level of feeling even more certain about our situation. The assurance we are describing here involves coherent and consistent assurance, an assurance that can be relied on. We are not speaking of just fooling yourself into thinking you are okay; rather, it's an assurance that parallels knowing.

When we do not feel assured, we worry, we fret, and we check and recheck. When we do these things, our progress suffers—rather than going forward, we become indecisive and wishy-washy.

Bladder/Uplifted

Being uplifted suggests that someone or something is holding us up and supporting us. To be uplifted is to have increased buoyancy. When we are lifted up, we can see beyond the strains and stresses of life.

In the case of the bladder, the thing that is lifting up—or doing the uplifting—is the muscles. The nutrient of the muscular system contains the quality of being teachable. The muscular system is willing to hold up the bladder (one of the parts of our bodies that we normally don't think much about, and when we do think about it, we generally regard it in an unpleasant sort of way). When our muscles are teachable, they continue to maintain and uplift. When the muscles no longer hold up the bladder, there is leakage and loss of function—accompanied by embarrassment—as support is withdrawn.

Nervous System/Gentleness

"Nothing is so strong as gentleness, nothing so gentle as real strength." **St. Francis de Sales**

Gentleness is underpinned by great strength; this strength stems in turn from being teachable and existing in a state of quality. Both of these attributes act the way the skeletal and muscular systems do when they support the nervous system—just as the gentleness commands strength, so does the nervous system command the entire body.

How nice that the nervous system's major nutrient is Gentleness. Gentleness might seem weak, but there is bold power behind it. When we think of our nervous system, which consists of the brain, spinal cord, and nerves, we realize that none of these specific things are strong; they are, in fact, highly fragile. The spinal cord has to be protected and sheathed by the bones surrounding it. In most cases, the nerves are encased deep within tissue. The brain is protected by the skull. If it weren't for the nervous system, however, we could not exist. Continuing to remain in a state of constant alertness and harmony requires great strength.

The nervous system is a giant communication network. Something can happen in a remote area of the body (say, the big toe) and our nervous system will immediately inform the entire body of what has happened. Help from many parts of the body rushes to the aid of the toe.

A lot of teamwork needs to happen within this system to make everything work together in harmony. Teamwork requires sensitivity and an ability to sense when something extra is needed; gentleness implies a softness and delicate nature that is sensitive to the needs of others. This is truly what the nervous system does for the body: it is a sensitive and delicate internal network. The nerves—although protected—are of a delicate nature. (Bruise a nerve or even touch a nerve when getting your teeth cleaned, and you'll find out just how delicate and sensitive the nerves are!) The spinal cord, too, is delicate and sensitive, working as it does to respond to the information coming in from all parts of the body and to then relay that information to the brain.

Although the nerves, the brain, and the spinal cord are delicate and sensitive—that is, gentle—they are supported by the strength and quality of the bones and the flexibility of the muscles. The synergy of these systems is what gives the body its ability to move and to sense its surroundings. The nervous system also decodes the stimuli coming in from the environment. Without a nervous system to interpret what we are seeing, hearing, feeling, tasting, and smelling, we would not be able to interact with the outside world or our inside environment.

How does gentleness feed and nourish the nervous system? We can sense a sharp, penetrating touch that brings pain…and we can experience a soft, soothing touch that brings pleasure. Sometimes a bit of pressure also feels good, but at a certain point, pressure becomes painful. These touches provide the nervous system with environmental input. A "touch" doesn't have to be physical, either. It can be emotional, mental, or spiritual. Painful contact will give the nervous system information about the environment, but will also bring trauma and stress to the body. A gentle touch carries no trauma.

What are some tools you can use to bring gentleness into your life?

Rabbit Moiety. This creation addresses both the emotional and spiritual field. A rabbit's natural disposition is tender-hearted and timid. It is easily frightened and self-sacrificing. It keenly feels outer exposure (say from foxes and predators) and inner pressure (its own defenselessness), and it is restless and vulnerable. Moiety means a part of the whole. The need for this moiety is present based on the perception an individual has of his or her environment. A moiety can be strung and worn as a necklace or be carried in a pocket on the left side of the body. Moieties are designed to be worn continuously during the day and will last up to two years. The moiety is composed of a blend of essential oils and herbs, with keratin and gemstones packaged together in either bone shells or natural seeds. These containers will not disturb the tone of the vibration. (Moieties are available from *www.burdickinstitute.com*.)

While <u>Skin Brushing</u> is stimulating to the skin and the lymphatic system, it's also a great tool for the nervous system—it unclogs pathways of information when the lymphatic system (Forgiveness) and skin (Truth) are addressed. Being forgiving and truthful allows for gentleness.

<u>Gentle Cell</u> is a formula that addresses the information in the cellular field as it relates to gentleness. Gentle Cell consists of Peace & Calming Essential Oil blend from Young Living Essential Oils and wild rose (a Bach flower essence). These are combined in equal parts and are not diluted. Feel free to combine this for yourself and remember to shake well before you apply this blend to your skin, otherwise it will separate. Remember, this is to be used externally on the skin. (This blend is also available from *www.burdickinstitute.com*.) Peace & Calming is described in the *Essential Desk Reference* (published by Essential Science Publishing) as "promoting relaxation and a deep sense of peace and emotional well-being, helping to dampen tensions and uplift spirits." In her book *Bach Flower Therapy: Theory and Practice*, Mechthild Scheffer states that "anyone taking wild rose will gradually feel his spirits revive and begin to live again." (Peace & Calming is a blend of essential oils that are available from *www.younglivingus.com*.)

Amazonite and Sapphire Gemstones worn together speak to the body of gentleness. Amazonite has the vibration of dignity while sapphires have the vibration of being powerful. Together, this vibration creates powerful dignity, which is a beautiful description of gentleness. Carry these stones in your left pocket. If you use wire to string them together, understand that the wire can change or block the vibration that you are trying to create. Just carrying the loose stones in your pocket will give your body the vibrations it needs.

Gentleness is the health-giving nutrient of the Nervous System.

Brain/Justice

We all want justice and fairness. This high desire is reflected in our American judicial system where we have laws in place to protect the *individual*.

Like a healthy judicial system, a healthy brain discerns between many choices and interests. The brain weighs the pros and cons, uses logic to make decisions, and arrives at a conclusion whose outcome often involves an intricate set of compromises and comparisons.

The brain is a complex organism that is not totally understood even by today's modern science. The brain receives information brought in through our senses, sorts out the signals, and ultimately makes its own sense of it all. Something that might seem totally fair to me might not be okay with your sense of fairness. When our sense of justice has been walked on, we feel this keenly. Even children are very aware of the sense of fairness.

Despair describes how we feel when justice has not been served. When there is injustice we rail against it.

BRAIN/JUSTICE

When we suffer injustices over and over again, we become confused and angry, even to the point of feeling crazy and unpredictable.

It will be a new day when we learn how to feed our prisoners and those who are suffering from mental illness the balance of nutrients that will heal them and restore their sense of justice.

Skeletal System/Quality

What is quality? Quality is defined in the dictionary as being fit, competent, or capable.

Our skeletal system holds us upright. Our skeletal system organizes our bodies. Our skeletal system provides our muscles with a strong foundation. Everything we do requires input from our skeletal system. Even while sleeping, our skeletal system is on alert—we toss, we turn, we rearrange our pillow. Just try getting out of bed without a skeletal system to support you!

Like all of our systems, our skeletal system is interdependent. Without input from the other systems, the skeletal system could not stand alone. (Pardon the pun…) When quality—or fitness—is not present in the body, we become less capable. The quality of our life suffers.

The skeletal system protects our internal organs from injury by moving us out of harm's way or by taking the brunt of an impact Typically, the day-to-day wear and tear on our skeletal system results from simple activities such as walking, jumping, running, sitting, or walking. We put stress on our skeletal system every day and think little about it…unless something gives way or breaks. (Generally speaking, our muscles will absorb the damage before a bone will break.)

Other connective tissues protect and support body tissues and internal organs. The human skeleton contains 206 bones, six of which are the tiny bones of the middle ear (three in each ear) that function in hearing. The largest bone in the body is the thigh bone or femur.

Mankind has endured many external conditions throughout the ages. From our modern-day perspectives, we would say that during much of this time, human life wasn't of very high quality…yet people's bones were intact. How does this fit into quality being the nutrient of the skeletal system? Well, even though we might feel that someone has a poor quality of life, the people who live in those environments don't think they do. They feel just as capable as you do—perhaps even more so. Their inner assurance of quality is what makes them strong and what makes their skeletal systems strong.

Are you suffering from a condition of the skeletal system? Ruptured discs occur as a result of a combination of problems from the nervous system, the muscular system, the skeletal system, and circulatory system. When we suffer a broken bone, the healing takes place whether we have the bone set or not. The unset bone will leave us with imperfections—in the gait, for instance, or the shape of the arm. Major surgery leaves its impression on the skin and the muscles. Even though our bodies mend well, we are left with scars from any intrusion into the skeletal system's territory.

Break a bone—any bone, even your little toe—and your quality of life will immediately suffer. Your ability to perform will be impaired. Break a major bone—like a leg bone—and you'll see how important your skeletal system is to your quality of life.

As we age, we feel less fit and capable. We believe that our bones have become thin and porous. Is this belief due to the actual aging process, or is it due to our belief that as we age our bodies MUST deteriorate? Our elders are very much afraid of breaking bones because their other systems are not optimally functioning and they know that this can lead to slow healing…or not healing at all. Could we say that our life quality also diminishes with aging? Our abilities wane. Our interests wane. A young person can take quite a hit before they break a bone, whereas an older person can turn their foot wrong and break an ankle. The elderly sometimes trip, fall, and break a hip. Some never recover from these injuries.

How do we obtain quality? When we are considering the health of our skeletal system, we need to consider the quality of our lives. What aspects of our lives give us quality? Some say that individual lifestyle choices drive the quality of life. Some say the quality of life is derived from the ones who love us. Some say the quality of life can be measured by how often we can go fishing. But the real answer is found in another question: which aspects of our lives make us fit and capable?

Someone said that there are three things in life that make life worth living. One is having something to do. Two is having someone to love. Three is having something to hope for. Having something to do is facilitated by our skeletal system—without it, we couldn't even lift a spoon to our mouth. **Our skeletal system makes us capable by translating our intentions into reality.** Whatever makes you feel capable and able in your life should be treasured.

Do you feel capable because you can bake the best apple pie? Then make apple pies and perfect each step of the process. Do you feel capable because you have mastered the clarinet? Keep playing it and increase your mastery. Do you believe you can succeed? All of these are tied to the quality of life. Your belief in your own body's capabilities—whether they're mental, physical, or spiritual—certainly dictates your quality of life. The old adage is true: if you think you can, you can. If you think you can't, you're still right.

How do we retain quality in our lives? Unless young children don't receive the proper nutrients for growth, it's rare for them to have problems with their skeletal system. Childhood is a time for growth, and the skeletal system usually chugs right along, even with all the demands that are placed upon it. Children love to run and play and jump and move—they never worry about not being able to do something.

Do you still believe you can do anything? Do you believe your body will support you? Or do you think you're too old, that you aren't as capable as you once were? Negative thoughts like these give the signal to the skeletal system to begin to break down.

What are some tools we can use to bring quality back into our lives and environment? How can we believe in our own capabilities again?

One valuable tool is exercise, which is a two-sided coin: we need to stop dreading it, and we need to stop being slaves to it. Moving the body is supposed to be joyful and fulfilling—it's not supposed to be a grind.

The reason we begin to believe we are less capable than someone else—or that we're less capable than our old selves used to be—is because we've stopped listening to our internal signals. Your body will tell you when you need to stop and when you need to move. Knowing that you're capable of this will make your movements spontaneous and fluid.

Many things on earth can naturally help us renew our belief in quality and capability. Here are some of the tools we can use to bring back those vibrations:

Purple. Wear it. If purple is too loud for you to wear in large swatches, buy purple socks and purple underwear.

When you put on your socks, let the color remind you that you are capable. Purple is the color of royalty. Don't just believe that you are royalty, KNOW that you are.

See the color purple by contacting an Aura Soma practitioner and obtaining liquid purple. You can mist this color into your aura, apply it to your neck, or apply it to any other areas where you feel a lack of mobility or fluidity.

Eat the color purple. Some suggestions for eating purple are eggplant, grapes, red cabbage, and plums.

Quality Savory is a blend of Bell Heather Flower Essence and citrine gemstones. Put the formula in the sun for four hours and then spray it into your aura. Bell Heather Flower Essence is from the Findhorn collection of flower essences in Scotland. Their literature tells us that bell heather's keynote is self-confidence: "Bell heather helps us to access inner strength and resolve to stand one's ground. We become resilient to stress, setback or disappointment when we remain flexible, consolidate our energies and stand firmly grounded and confident in ourselves." Citrine gemstones speak to us of embracing truth. This formula appeals to the sense of taste, which translates to hope in the etheric body. You can blend this yourself as noted above, or you can order it from *www.burdickinstitute.com*.

Quality Tactile addresses the need for touch. In the etheric body, touch translates as forgiveness. Take a large, flat wooden stick—like a tongue depressor or a popsicle stick—and use some glue to attach dried millet and tanzanite stones. Wave this through your aura to strengthen your skeletal system, taking special care to address painful, sore areas in the body. The Quality Tactile is available from *www.burdickinstitute.com* or feel free to create this tactile on your own.

Quality Triz. This blend of essential oils, herbs, and gemstones comprises the vibration of quality. They have been placed in a square glass cube and are designed to be placed by your bed or wherever you will be spending most of your time. The portable triz is a small one-inch by one-inch cube whose vibrations last up to four years and can be placed in your pocket so you can take it with you and have the vibrational effect as you go through your day. The herbal ingredients in the Quality Triz are butcher's broom, asparagus root, and flaxseeds. The gemstones in the Quality Triz are Herkimer diamonds. The essential oils in the Quality Triz are Citrus Fresh, Endoflex, Juniper and Acceptance. These are proprietary blends available from Young Living Essential Oils.

Diamond Gem Elixirs contain the vibration of quality and can be used to enhance the vibration of quality in your life. Available from *www.alaskanessences.com* and other flower essence companies. Alaskan Essences has this to say about Diamond Gem Elixir: "Healing Qualities—brings clarity to the 6th chakra; helps us see through illusion; harmonizes Divine and personal will; helps us activate personal will in its highest form; strengthens the ability to act in alignment with our Divine purpose."

SKELETAL SYSTEM/QUALITY

Some <u>essential oils</u> containing the vibration of quality are basil, frankincense, and valerian. See section 2 for information on the messages of these essential oils.

Some <u>flowers</u> containing the message of quality are poppies, apple blossoms, cherry blossoms, and Indian paintbrush.

Quality is the health-giving nutrient of the Skeletal System.

Muscular System/Teachable

In seconds, our muscles must react to multiple stimuli. Our body's response could be a startled jump (prompted by a loud noise), or a slide into sleep (when someone smoothes our hair and strokes our head). Depending on the need and situation, our muscles adapt and flex.

Our muscles also respond to the nervous system. When we touch a hot stove, nerves send a danger message to our muscles, which then prompt us to instantly pull our hand back. Our muscles are "taught" by the entire body and by many different environments. They must be flexible and alert at all times.

"Teachable" is described in the dictionary as the state of being capable of being taught. To teach is to give instruction, to inform, and to make understood.

Athletes have taken the ability of the muscles to a whole new level. Whether they're gymnasts, swimmers, skiers, or shot-putters, we marvel when we watch athletes perform. These people have spent their entire lives training their muscles to respond and succeed at their individual sports, where sometimes the timing of a millisecond can make the difference between winning and losing.

As athletes train, their bodies and muscles become strong and resilient. If their muscles were inflexible—resisting and fighting back—injuries would occur. Sprained and strained muscles mean that the athlete has to take time out from his or her sport to allow the muscles to repair themselves.

When you are teachable you are still flexible and ready for new input. You're willing to take new steps and use new information to "exercise." When we can no longer be taught, we become rigid and fixed. Old ideas can keep us from moving forward. As the saying goes, "A man convinced against his will is of the same opinion still." Rigidity and inflexibility are the bane of muscles. As we age, we lose our ability to move freely and quickly, and instead we become stiff and sore. After we've sat for a while—such as after a long car ride—we moan when we attempt to move again. Our agility is no longer what it used to be.

As we age, we tend to reject new ideas and information. "We've never done it that way before," we say. "What is this world coming to? The old ways are the best ways." But our lives are not meant to be stagnant; we should not be unable to absorb new information. When we find ourselves resisting change, we find ourselves becoming unteachable, rigid, and inflexible.

How do we remain teachable and flexible? How do we remain open to new ideas, able to give up our old ones if necessary? One of the ways we can do this is to acknowledge that change is necessary for growth and flexibility: if we sit in a chair for years, we won't be able to get out of the chair.

When I was five years old, I had to be in the hospital. I was not allowed to get out of bed for any reason. When I was allowed to get up again months later, my legs felt like rubber—they buckled with every step. I remember being amazed that they would not support me. Fortunately it didn't take long for my muscles to remember what they were supposed to be doing…and fortunately I was anxious to get out and run and play again. But often we lose our desire to play, and that's when we become inflexible. Moving toward change with trust and confidence is inviting change and learning, and sometimes that is the very thing we fear.

So to keep our muscular systems strong, we need to remain open and ready for change. When we walk, for example, our muscles have to adjust and change every instant. They have to be adaptable and open to signals from our nervous systems and our brains. When our brains cannot provide instruction to the muscular system, the muscles can't move. When they can't be "taught," they are inflexible and cannot function.

Here are some tools to bring in the nutrient of being teachable.

Royal Blue Pomander from Aura Soma. Royal Blue is described as being a perception-strengthener, one that exposes you to the powers of your imagination and intuition. It also helps you access sympathetic emotions. Royal Blue Pomander is available from an Aura Soma practitioner.

The Teachable Mandala consists of sapphires, turquoise, tourmaline, emeralds, and peridot gemstones. Sapphires denote powerfulness. Turquoise encourages the knowledge that there is a cure and the ability to accept it. Tourmaline prompts us to look forward. Emeralds speak to us of compassion, and peridots give us a fresh perspective. Together, the message is that you are powerful, able to effect change, forward-looking, compassionate, and have a fresh and unbiased perspective. All of these are only possible if we are teachable and open to change. The gemstones are arranged in the shape of a circle to represent timelessness and eternity. Mandalas are available from *www.burdickinstitute.com* or feel free to create your own. Remember to use only cotton, silk, or Niobium wire to string these gemstones together. Metals block the vibrations of the gemstones.

The Teachable Savory consists of willow herb and topaz. Willow herb is a flower essence while topaz is a gemstone. Combine them with sunlight for four hours and then use the mixture as an auric spray to affect the unconscious level of energy in the etheric body. Willow herb's key note is self-mastery: "Willow herb helps to balance authoritarian or overbearing behaviors by tempering these forces with true power. The responsible integration of will and power is brought about by love and humility." (This excerpt is taken from the Findhorn Flower Essences information.) Topaz gemstone encourages us to continue to grow and not fall into a rut. The line of savory formulations are designed to address the etheric body's sense of hope.

New Zealand Dandelion Flower Essence "addresses muscular tension—especially in the neck, shoulders, and back—for rigid-thinking people whose attitudes tend towards 'delay,' 'refer,' or 'consider.' These people often see no good in any given situation. Dandelion flower essence helps release tension, allowing the soul to experience a more balanced flow of energy from inner emotions to outer body functions. This is a good essence for over-achievers—it brings relaxation to their constant on-the-go lives." Positive qualities: zest/lively activity, inner balance, easing tension. This flower essence is available from *www.essencesonline.com.*

Being teachable is the health-giving nutrient of the Muscular System.

Digestive System/Temperance

What is temperance? The dictionary says that temperance "is the state or quality of being moderate in action, speech, or habits." In other words, temperance is self-control. And what is the meaning of "moderate"? Again, the dictionary to the rescue: "proper restraint; within limits." We should have known!

The Digestive System is an overarching system that includes several specific organs. Some of the organs and glands in the body have multiple capacities in multiple systems—the thyroid, for example, plays a role in the reproductive system, the endocrine system, and the digestive system. Because of this multiplicity of function, in order to understand how temperance forms the main nutrient of the digestive system, we need to look at the whole package. Here's a flow chart of the digestive system's main components:

Digestive System: Temperance and Self-Control
<u>Bucal cavity (including teeth, saliva, etc.):</u>
At ease, relaxed, relieved

(Are we ever uptight when we eat?)
<u>Throat and esophagus:</u>
Mastery and control
(Suggests martyrdom when function is impaired)
<u>Stomach:</u>
Strength
(Impaired digestion suggests weakness)
<u>Liver:</u>
Stability
(Do we ever experience instability in the form of being wishy-washy?)
<u>Small Intestines:</u>
Highly valued
(Do we ever think, "I'm not enough" or "I'm insignificant"?)
<u>Colon:</u>
Authenticity

(Sometimes we think we can't be ourselves because we believe that self to be unacceptable)

The digestive system—or temperance or self-control—includes all the elements of the digestive system. The sufferings that may come from our digestive system can be seen in the above chart. A healthy digestive system is one that exercises self-control and proper restraint.

To achieve this, food should be met in a relaxed atmosphere—i.e., whatever we choose to eat should not be accompanied by a side of doubt and guilt. Choose your food wisely, and then send the food on its way with mastery and control. Remember: we are not controlled BY what we eat, we CONTROL what we eat. We have the strength to utilize what we have decided to consume. Stability in our lives results from our choices. We value ourselves highly and choose wisely. We are authentic. We are ourselves. We are happy with who we are.

What is the digestive system? The digestive system consists of the organs and glands in the body responsible for digestion. The digestive system begins with the mouth and extends through the esophagus, stomach, small intestine, and large intestine. It ends with the rectum and anus. Other organs in this system include the liver, pancreas, gallbladder, and appendix.

How do we obtain temperance? It's an age-old question. Although many think of temperance as being willpower, it really isn't. Temperance stems from learning to value ourselves, and in doing so, we obtain temperance (or willpower). But how do we learn to value ourselves? These are questions that have been posed for generations; psychologists have labored for centuries to help people solve this dilemma. How do we value ourselves when we've grown up to think that we're not of value?

> *"What is a weed? A plant whose virtues have not yet been discovered."* **Ralph Waldo Emerson**

Learning to value ourselves requires the use of knowledge and truth: the knowledge that your true self has been demeaned and repressed and the stark truth of realizing that you do not value yourself. To arrive at a new truth, you need to rewrite the primary knowledge: "That was then. This is now. NOW I value myself. TODAY I am able to be authentic." Some adults cannot be their true selves because they think that doing so would threaten their partner. Indeed, learning to value yourself might cause quite an upheaval in your circumstances and in your life. Do you value yourself enough to risk that?

Keep temperance in your life. Continue to value YOU. How do you maintain that value in the midst of many voices of dissent? You have the choice to listen to those voices. Don't. Listen to your own inner voice. Only YOU have the right to judge yourself because only YOU know all the facts and motives and desires that have brought you to your present state. Forgive what needs to be forgiven. Forget what needs to be forgotten. Value yourself enough to take positive steps and reinforce your value. Regardless of what has happened in the past, it's the past. Let it go. Start fresh and stay fresh.

Some tools to bring temperance and self-value into your environment:

Affirmations:

*I set myself free. I am forgiven. I have a clean slate.
I am anticipating good things in my life.
I am expecting good things in my life.
All good things flow freely to me and through me.
I see myself in a new light of love.
There is no limit to my value. I am priceless.*

Put these affirmations where you will see them every day. Type them out and put them on your fridge, hang them above your sink in the kitchen and bathroom, hang them above your washing machine. Allow yourself to ponder their meaning, and when you feel some resistance to the message, ask yourself, "Why?" Then recognize how you have devalued yourself and change your internal perception of yourself to be one of value. Affirmations affect us on the highest level of being, the level where our guides and angels reside. Words are the most powerful tool mankind possesses.

Temperance Wisdom Sachets reinforce your inner value. This combination has been especially designed for the digestive system and includes burdock root, feverfew, elderberries, and eyebright, along with Exodus II and Magnify Your Purpose essential oils. The herbs and essential oils are in packets so that you can put them in your pocket and carry them with you all day. They have vibrations to feed your digestive system. Wisdom Sachets work on the level of the soul. Wisdom Sachets are available from www.burdickinstitute.com or feel free to create your own.

Temperance Jemmie Stones are a collection of gemstones that speaks to your value. It includes citrine (embracing truth), topaz (getting out of a rut), tourmaline (looking forward), tanzanite (resolute), and amethyst (joyful). These are all messages to help you stay on track to value yourself. Put them in a little pouch and take them with you wherever you go. Gemstones work on the level of the spirit. Gemstones can be found in various rock and gem shops and online.

The <u>Shake Hands–Crocus</u> blend of essential oils is designed to give the body permission to experience peace, to feel fulfilled, to be optimistic, and to shrug off burdens. The words "shake hands" indicate that this information has been accepted only after a struggle. The struggle consisted of feeling indecisive—as though there was no way out, as though there was no way to be except introverted and withdrawn. All of these situations are indicative of feeling worthless. Let's throw away that negative set of values and shake hands with our new way of being. This blend has been processed on the Terra Spun[1] to give it an electrical charge, which in turn allows this formula to affect your body's emotional field of information. These blends work on that level.

Temperance is the health-giving nutrient of the Digestive System.

---

[1]

Colon/Authenticity

Can you be yourself? Can you be your real self? Are you allowed to be who you are and are you honored for who you are? If you say no to any of these questions, you may be experiencing problems with your colon.

To have a healthy colon, we need to be authentic. We need to be who we really are—and we need to be who we really are without apology.

When we can't be authentic because someone doesn't approve of us or we don't like who we are—or we're ashamed of ourselves—we can feel the effects of this negativity in the pit of our stomachs and in our bowels. This is the feeling we get when we have a dream that we're sitting in class naked, or when we have to give a speech and we're unprepared, or when we have to interact with someone who doesn't like us. We get this nauseous feeling because we fear the experience of not being authentic. When we deny our true self, we bring unrest to the colon and to the entire digestive system.

Liver/Stability

In order to build a house, it has to have a foundation—if it doesn't, the walls and the roof will fall in. The liver behaves much like the foundation of a house, supporting the functions of the body. Since the liver is so critical to the health and maintenance of the body, any instability or liver issue affects the whole body.

Stability gives us a platform, a base for operations. Stability is solid. It's something we can count on.

When we're unstable, we're unsteady and unreliable. We can't walk very far and we certainly can't run. In short, everything becomes a chore. None of us wants to become unstable.

Small Intestines/Highly Valued

Most of us don't think about the true value of our intestines. We don't realize that the intestines and colon make up a large part of our immune system. Food is carried through the walls of the small intestine before it is absorbed into the blood and carried to every organ, gland, and system in our bodies.

Our small intestine's worth cannot be overrated. Not only does it contribute to the health of our immune system, but it also nourishes the entire body by providing it with nutrition that can be absorbed and used. The small intestine protects us and feeds us; it also cleanses us by allowing waste to pass through and out of the body.

To be highly valued suggests that something is valued beyond the normal sense of the word. When we place a high value upon something, we keep it safe. We might insure it or even put it in a safety deposit box at the bank to be certain it's protected.

To be highly valued is the nutrient of our small intestine—how we feel about ourselves has a direct bearing on its health.

Stomach/Strength

Strength: a very prized attribute. Having strength allows us to persevere through hard times, to enjoy recreation, to experiences the pleasures of building and working.

The stomach depends on a substance called hydrochloric acid to break down substances for digestion. If you have ever thrown up, you're familiar with the power of hydrochloric acid—it can burn! Many people have acid reflux, which is what occurs when the acid in the stomach backs up in the esophagus. This can be a serious problem because the esophagus can become scarred from the constant exposure to hydrochloric acid.

If this acid is present anywhere in the body except the stomach, it can cause acute problems. The stomach, however, has resiliency and strength—layers upon layers of tissue retain the contents of the stomach and protect the body from being damaged by leaked acid.

Reproductive System/Faith

What is the reproductive system? It is a system of organs and glands and parts that play a vital role in reproduction. In the male, this system consists of the testes, penis, seminal vesicles, prostate, and urethra. In the female, the reproductive system consists of the ovaries, fallopian tubes, uterus, and vagina.

What is faith? Basically, it's trust. Trust and faith are listed as synonymous in the dictionary. Each describes the other. Faith is belief coupled with conviction and accomplished through experience.

There are things we trust and things we don't trust. How do we decide which is which?

Unless we're talking about a newborn baby, our trust cannot be established without proof. Trust comes from experience—for example, we trust that the sun will come up each morning. It has done so for as long as we can remember, before we had history or even legends. We simply trust that the sun will come up. Faith, on the other hand, is not something we have because of the absence or presence of proof—we believe in our faith because of what we have experienced.

When a mother or a father asks a child to jump into her or his arms, usually the child will jump. But if you ask them to jump into the arms of a total stranger, they will not…or, if they do, they jump with great hesitancy.

If a person with whom you've had bad experiences asked you for a favor, you'd probably hesitate, but if someone you know and trust asks you for a favor, you would do it…and probably with joy. You don't have absolute proof that they will "repay" you, but you have faith that they will.

We can see that faith does not believe without proof; rather, it is belief coupled with conviction and accomplished through experience. Faith is knowledge that comes from the experience behind the trust.

How do we obtain faith? We obtain faith through experience.

When my husband and I got married, I didn't know how he would react to every experience. There have been many times when I've questioned his actions and wondered about his motives. But now—after thirty-three years together—I have great faith in him. I know him. I trust him. He is a man of integrity: if he says something, he will follow through. I know that he loves me even though I had questioned that early on in our relationship. He has come through the hardest test of a marriage—losing a child—and he has never wavered in his support of and love for me. He has shown me that I can trust him.

"The power of love to change bodies is legendary, built into folklore, common sense, and everyday experience. Love moves the flesh, it pushes matter around... Throughout history, 'tender loving care' has uniformly been recognized as a valuable element in healing." Larry Dossey

But obtaining experience can be a fearful and scary expedition. Do we dare embark on that journey? There is no other way to obtain faith. We have to step onto the path and have trust in the outcome. This is how faith relates to the reproductive system. Embarking upon the journey of parenthood can entail many long years. Do we have faith in our partner? Do we have faith that the ones we are ushering into the world will want to be here? That they—like us—will be taken care of?

What have we told our children about the earth's ability to sustain us? Think about what we as a culture currently believe in the United States. Don't we all think that we're going to perish—and probably soon? There are terrorists. There is global warming. There is disease. How can we trust a world like this? But these are merely thought patterns that we have all been supporting. If we support another paradigm, our cultural beliefs can change.

There is evidence of this change in the hard-fought struggle couples are having with conception: fertility clinics now abound. The presence of so many fertility problems on such a large scale is a new phenomenon in our day and generation. Never before have we lost so much faith in our future as human beings.

We have all heard of couples wanting to have children and trying for years and years to conceive. They finally give up, adopt, and…whoa, they become pregnant! They have turned away from their worry (which destroys trust) and have stopped trying to control the outcome. This is because their bodies can then relax and trust, and the reproductive system starts to operate normally again. Faith—which includes a lack of worry—is our natural, healthy state.

When a woman reaches menopause, she begins to worry. She wonders, "Am I beautiful enough to hold my husband when all around me there are women much younger and much more desirable? What are these wrinkles and these bulges?" We experience hot flashes and accompanying panic, things that we've never experienced before. But what we're doing differently is this: we are playing host to worry and fear.

After a while, our hot flashes will subside and stop. This is because we see that life goes on. We (usually) are not dumped for a younger model, and people do not shun us. On the contrary, we realize that we had shunned ourselves. In time, we learn to accept the new person we have become. This acceptance comes with hard-won experience. Women in many other countries avoid this step—as we wish we could—because their cultures value the wisdom of the older generations. Knowledge, they believe, comes with age.

How do we maintain faith in our lives? How do we strive to obtain more faith? A wise man once said, "Consider all the things you are worrying about. Imagine the worst that could happen and decide how you would react and what you would do in that situation. Then realize that you have done all you can and let your worries go." Most of us know that we can't plan for every eventuality. Things are going to happen that we haven't anticipated.

If you look back at your life, you'll see that everything that has happened led to something else. You couldn't have planned it and orchestrated it better. Even so-called "bad" things can result in unexpected treasures and life lessons. Some gifts have come through the darkness of the soul.

Use each day to build upon what you have already experienced. It's almost certain that the sun will come up in the morning, for example. Likewise, if your step falters or you miss it altogether, experience has proven that you'll be okay. You'll continue to be okay and loved.

We can trust that there is a higher purpose for our lives that we can't fully comprehend right now. Before we have children, we can't understand how we will love them. After all, we don't even know them. We hope we will have enough love for them, that we will be what they need to grow and flourish. That when they arrive, love will take over our hearts, and that after years have gone by, we won't be able to fathom how we lived without them.

What are some tools you can use to bring faith into your environment? Faith, remember, is brought about by experience. Experience is brought about by doing. Try some of these exercises. Gain experience through them and see how those experiences can bring faith and trust into your life.

Faith Triz. This triz box is designed create the vibration of faith through the use of essential oils, herbs, and flower essences that speak this message. The Faith Triz contains Sara essential oil. The message of this oil is that you are esteemed, chaste, refreshed, and innocent. This triz also contains Aroma Siez, which contains the message that you are yielding, flowing, restored, and at ease. Colloidal silver's message is you are loved. The Faith Triz also contains eyebright. Eyebright speaks of justice. Calendula's message is you are priceless. The Faith Triz also contains moonstone and onyx gemstones. Moonstone encourages us to be outgoing while onyx speaks to us of skill. Thus, the combined message addresses all the fears and concerns we would have about faith and going forward in life, about trusting that everything in our lives will work out. Here is the complete message: "You are applauded, chaste, refreshed, and innocent. You are yielding, flowing, restored, and at ease. You are loved. There is justice. You are priceless. You are outgoing and skilled." This combination of essential oils, herbs and gemstones is enclosed and sealed in a square glass cube. The square cube speaks of completion. Feel free to create this Faith Triz for yourself (or order it from our website at *www.burdickinstitute.com*).

Pearl Gem Elixir. Remember the truth contained within a pearl: it is through the constant irritation the sand brings about in the shell that the oyster creates the beautiful pearl. Pearls, then, are born of tribulation. Faith is created through experience. The Pearl Gem Elixir from Alaskan Essences states: "Healing Qualities: helps one process and dissolve layers of irritation that have built up in the mental and emotional bodies and manifest in the physical body as hardness and inflexibility; helps turn antagonism toward oneself and criticism or judgment of one's illness into acceptance and understanding." (Available from Alaska Flower Essences.)

The Faith Mandala is designed to create the vibration of faith. It consists of quartz, turquoise, rhodochrosite, amethyst, and citrine. These gemstones have been combined in a circle to represent timelessness. Feel free to create your own mandala (or find it on our website at *www.burdickinstitute.com*).

Petrified Forest Flower Essence and Ancient Forest Flower Essences. Long, long ago, these fossilized remnants of the ancient forests of Arizona lived and breathed. Their essence breaks up rigid and crystallized patterns in one's emotional, mental, and spiritual life, healing and releasing petrified fear. They are wonderful for any type of energy/bodywork. (Available through *www.essencesonline.com* .[2][3])

Faith is the health-giving nutrient of the Reproductive System.

2
3

Uterus/Consciousness

Women are great sensors. Even if there is no immediate proof, women's intuition tells us when everything is all right or if something is amiss. It's a sure knowing, a feeling that we can trust.

This knowing and sensing is what defines consciousness as a nutrient. The dictionary tells us that consciousness is the ability to know and sense your outside world, through seeing, feeling, hearing, or otherwise sensing something, either physically or emotionally.

Testes/Self-Esteem

Self-esteem is the feeling of being able to play at the peak of the game. It's the rush and exhilaration of being at the top. It is the feeling of exhilaration when you are feeling on top of the world.

Self-esteem is the nutrient of the testes—it's when a man feels that everything is possible and the world is his oyster. He loves life and believes in himself.

Ovaries/Optimism

Similar to the self-esteem of the testes, the nutrient of the ovaries is optimism, believing that everything is possible, that only good lies ahead, and that life is worth living.

Prostate/Invigorated and Productive

Being invigorated and feeling energized and alive. A productive feeling that you can get things done and will soon enjoy the fruits of your labor.

Wow, life can conspire to counteract those feelings of feeling invigorated and productive. It's time for you to retire, you're too old. You're too forgetful. You can't keep up. All these messages, spoken or silent, can be very detrimental for the prostate.

Lymphatic System/Forgiveness

What is forgiveness? The dictionary says that forgiveness is to give up the wish to punish or "get even" with others; to not have hard feelings at or toward others; to pardon, absolve, and excuse others for their actions. Forgiveness allows us to give up all claims to something, to not demand payment, or to forgive a debt.

Forgiveness is really the ability to stay connected to our true selves.

When we feel wronged by someone, we want to remove them from our lives as soon as possible. This is not forgiveness—this is avoidance. Someone else has made us feel wrong, and dealing with this internal sense of feeling we are wrong is what we're avoiding.

What is the lymphatic system? The lymphatic system is a network of small vessels and tissue spaces that move lymph throughout the body. The lymphatic system has several functions, including filtering out harmful bacteria, manufacturing white blood cells (white blood cells are produced by the lymph nodes), distributing nutrients to the cells of the body, helping maintain the body's fluid balance by draining off excess fluids so that tissues do not swell, and assisting in the digestion of fats.

Four steps lead to forgiveness.

Step One:
The first step toward forgiveness is stepping outside of yourself and seeing the big picture. It is important to look at your situation with mercy and a heart ready for acceptance. Tune into your inner self and see what is relevant or part of the forgiveness process and acknowledge those parts of the situation that are not part of the process. Suddenly, instead of seeing the micro-situation and focusing on the tiny pebble in your shoe, you've opened the door, stepped outside, and now noticed that the world is full of pebbles and that one happens to be in your shoe. Step One in forgiveness is seeing what the true situation is—i.e., viewing it from a broader perspective. If you can step outside of yourself, you will see that your current situation, too, will pass. You will endure beyond this tiny pinpoint in time that you—and you alone—have chosen to hone in on. This focus was totally your choice.

You will also begin to see what has comprised the need for forgiveness. It's sufficient to recognize it for what it is—you don't need to harp on it and add to it a long string of past insults. Your current situation is just a pebble in your shoe. The sore toe you already have is from another incident—it's not related to this one.

LYMPHATIC SYSTEM/FORGIVENESS

When you look at the situation with mercy and a big heart, the view becomes clearer. Mercy is something you probably don't deserve but have likely been granted many times. This is a tool of love that you can extend to yourself. No, maybe you don't deserve mercy, but in offering it to yourself, you can free yourself. Mercy lets go of judgment and steps in when judgment fails. Extend this magical eraser to yourself.

Lastly, become attuned. When you are attuned, you exist in harmony with yourself and others. Discord occurs because two or more notes are being played that do not blend. If you play each note by itself, it sounds fine. Start to play the notes one at a time until you can hear how they can blend harmoniously.

Step Two:
Step Two involves comprehension, empathy, creation, and reconciliation. Comprehending or understanding why we feel hurt moves us in the direction of forgiveness. Empathy is feeling for another; it's feeling what they feel. Take a moment and feel—really experience what you are feeling. What is that? Is it envy? Is it anger? The only person you can effectively change is yourself, so try to feel what YOU are feeling.

Part of Step Two is becoming creative and working toward reconciliation. "Creating" usually involves making something that has not been in the physical world before, but the new solution you will create will be a structure in your internal world, a place where you can store your feelings and visions. Do you currently house those feelings in a rundown shack, shameful and hidden from view? House your new understanding in a mansion. There, you can tell others the story of its creation and how your ugly duckling became a swan.

Can you describe your initial reaction to the situation? Perhaps at first you didn't see any positive potential within it, but then—after reflection and focus—you could see the situation reshaping itself into a beautiful creation that you can now share with everyone. Could this be one of the most beautiful opportunities you've had in your life? And to think that you almost missed the beauty in that experience!

Now we've come to reconciliation. Reconciliation is a result of making an active settlement or adjustment. Settling occurs when something has shifted and changed. This means that what was "that" before has now become "this." "This" is the new thing you have created. Make it beautiful.

Step Three:
How do you keep forgiveness in your life? Step Three deals with reunion, going forward, and unity. Reuniting with your true self allows you to come into contact with that part of your being that bears no grudges or resentments.

Your true self does not want to punish others and extract payment from them—your true self wants to live in harmony with yourself and the world around you. This true self can now take strong, assured, unencumbered steps into the future. Stay connected with this true self.

Step Four:
Step Four consists of production and winning. Production is what results from work—i.e., effort being put forth. Taking the steps of forgiveness has produced a result. If you have taken all of these steps and now are at Step Four, you are conquering the struggle. You can now stride past your struggles without the past dragging at your heels. You are free.

To review, here are the four steps again:

Step outside of your small focus and see the big picture.

> *Understand and really feel what's in your own heart. Create something beautiful from this new comprehension.*

Reunite with your true self.

Enjoy the results of having conquered your struggles.

How does forgiveness relate to the lymphatic system? Allow us to lay a little groundwork for support and understanding regarding this connection in the following explanation.

Our lymphatic system is like a second blood system in the way it functions and looks—it's connected to almost every part of our body. If you could see a model of it, it would look like an internal networking system.

The lymph fluid begins as blood plasma in the bloodstream. From the blood plasma—which carries the body's nutrients through the capillaries, or small veins—the plasma leaves the capillaries and becomes known as intercellular or interstitial fluid. The interstitial fluid delivers nutrients, oxygen, and hormones to the cells. There, the interstitial fluid collects and carries away cellular waste products. Most of the tissue fluid returns to the capillary bed, becomes plasma, and continues as venous circulation. Ten percent of the tissue fluid is left behind—this ten percent left behind is what comprises lymph fluid. The amount of lymph circulating in the body is one to two quarts and makes up one to three percent of the body's total weight.

The role of lymph is to take out the trash and to dispose of it by circulating between the cells and collecting waste products as it goes.

As it absorbs dissolved protein, the lymph becomes rich in protein. One-way valves within the lymphatic capillaries ensure the continued flow of the lymph away from the tissues.

What happens in our lymphatic systems is in close alignment with what happens when we forgive…and when we don't forgive.

Forgiveness only flows in one direction; likewise, we can't expect an outsider to clean our being. Forgiveness is something we have to do for ourselves. The established flow is out and away, and when this doesn't happen, lymph fluid is retained. When we don't forgive, resentments, hurts, and slights build up inside of us.

Forgiveness is the substance that allows for the removal of waste. This waste is a natural function of living and taking in food, water, and air. Forgiveness is required in our everyday lives. When we can forgive, it is simply another seamless function in the body—but when the perception of past hurts and slights accumulates, there is an unwillingness to let go, and even an inability to let go.

On a physical level, when the lymph fluid is backed up there is pain, swelling, and loss of function. When we don't forgive, pain and remorse become our unwanted teachers. When lymph is backed up and not flowing freely in the body, we begin to lose our ability to move forward; the steps we do take are painful and slow. This parallels closely with the emotional, spiritual pain of unforgiveness.

> *"God does not judge you according to your bodies and appearances, but He looks into your hearts and observes your deeds."* **The Qur'an (Koran)**

Movement is required to keep the lymph circulating. Humility and becoming teachable—which are the nutrients of the muscular system—are required for forgiveness. Forgiveness is closely aligned with our progress in experiencing joy and creativity. (See the chapter on joy.) The circulatory system (Joy), the lymph system (Forgiveness), and the respiratory system (Love) are intertwined.

When we don't forgive, our ability to experience joy and love suffers. When we don't have much joy or love in our lives, it is harder to forgive. On the other hand, when we are joyful, little slights and bumps hardly affect us. When we feel loved and joyful, then forgiving comes easily and without effort.

When we have extended forgiveness and created something beautiful out of the experience, every part of our experience is enriched. This is much like the protein-rich lymph.

And here are some tools to help us with this work of forgiveness.

Forgiveness Triz. This is a blend of essential oils, herbs, and gemstones that comprise the vibration of forgiveness. The Forgiveness Triz contains the herbs Isatis, FuLing, and Dulse. It also contains the essential oils of Valor and frankincense. The gemstones peridot, chrysoprase, and sapphires also comprise the Forgiveness Triz. This combination has been placed in a square glass cube representing completion. The Forgiveness Triz is designed to be placed by your bed or wherever you will be spending time of several hours. The vibrational benefit from the portable triz boxes will last approximately four years.

Quartz crystals have the frequency of forgiveness. Not only can they infuse or bring in the frequency of forgiveness, they can also transmit or broadcast this vibration to others. Carry them in your pocket. If you can't feel any help from them, increase the number that you keep with you. Remember to cleanse them at least every ten days—more often if you are in stressful situations—by rinsing them under cold running water for two or more minutes. Quartz crystals are available at rock shops and gem stores. You can also check online for sources.

Shake Hands–Daffodils. This is a blend of herbs and essential oils that has been charged and processed on the Terra Spun Device[i]. Shaking hands refers to the agreement of two opposing forces—when they agree, opposing forces can become allies. The opposing force addressed in Shake Hands –Daffodil is permissiveness. Permissiveness allows influences to stay in your life—even if they're negative—because you may have to deal with something worse if you were to remove those influences. The positive aspects of the handshake are orderliness and organization.

How does this relate to the forgiveness nutrient? When we make a conscious decision to discard unnecessary things, we re-instate a positive flow in our lives and create a clean and orderly environment in which we can work. Shake Hands–Daffodil is designed to be applied to the skin and comes in a roll-on bottle for convenience. It can be used multiple times a day without adverse effects and is safe for children and animals. (Available from *www.burdickinstitute.com.*)

Forgiveness is also closely aligned with touch. When we are harboring unforgiveness, being touched can be repulsive. Unforgiveness makes us want to withdraw and turn inward. This is why massage, reflexology, and acupressure are good ways to move lymph along in its vessels and are a wonderful way to help the body with forgiveness. (One specific therapy is called lymphatic massage.) These techniques are very helpful when lymph fluid has accumulated in the tissues. When we are bogged down, sluggish, and swollen, this fluid needs to be moved along and out. Touch is a useful tool for the work of forgiveness.

> *Forgiveness is the health-giving nutrient of the Lymphatic System.*

Integumentary System/Truth

What a wonderful creation our skin is! It stretches over our entire body, and our pores, sweat glands, hair, moles, freckles, rashes, and calluses are exposed to the world every moment of every day.

Not only is the skin a beautiful covering for our bodies, it protects our internal environment from the external environment. The skin can be cut, punctured, and burned, and yet will still repair itself. It can be sliced off and replanted in another part of the anatomy where it will re-grow. The skin protects us from the elements and acts as a sensor to transmit heat and cold, pain and pleasure.

How does all of this relate to the skin's nutrient of truth? Truth is resilient. It stands the test of time in a way that nothing else can. After many years of confusion and darkness, truth will triumph. Truth is one of the sensors we use to determine the validity of something. We often get goose bumps—or, as one of my friends says, truth bumps—when we hear something profoundly true. The term "thin-skinned" refers to someone who is overly sensitive; "thick-skinned," on the other hand, means someone who can let remarks slide off of them easily.

The skin can harbor some toxins and these can manifest as moles, skin tags, and liver spots. They're like little toxic waste dumps that are relegated to the skin's jurisdiction until our bodies can take care of them. (Some discolorations on the skin can be eliminated.) These little toxic waste dumps are distortions of truth—often, our bodies allow them to remain in place until we can see things in a different light…or until something is used on the skin (i.e., essential oils) that can absorb the distortions. Time changes our perceptions: we all have had the experience of being absolutely certain that something was true until life's experiences show us otherwise. Only then do we change our minds.

The skin also has sweat glands whereby the body is able to secrete waste products through the skin. This is why the skin is often referred to as being the "third kidney." Sweat also cools the body and regulates its temperature. People who have blood sugar issues often sweat profusely; when menopausal women experience hot flashes, they often sweat. Some thyroid issues cause sweating.

One of the plagues of youth is acne—it's mostly seen in teenagers and people in their twenties. We don't see as much of it as we used to; nowadays, prescription drugs are deployed to fight the bacteria that supposedly causes such breakouts. These breakouts, however, are nothing more than manifestations of the body trying to sort out the truth of its internal environment based on the signals it's receiving from its external environment.

The external environment for a teenager can be brutal: "You're ugly. You're stupid." Some kids hear this every day, and their skin reflects this abuse. After the high school years, these violent skin eruptions usually calm down. That's not surprising—skin reflects our body's internal environment. In our youth—and during important crossroads in life—our internal environments surge with doubts and fears. This surging and upheaval is due to the relentless assault of the external environments. Our hormones—which are the body's messengers—convey information to the organs and glands, information that is distorted because our inner truth is being challenged by our external environment.

To review:

The skin covers and protects our internal environment. Truth covers and protects our innermost being.

The skin is resilient and senses hot and cold, pain and pleasure. Truth is resilient and allows us to sense things that don't ring true.

The skin can harbor toxins. Truth can harbor little untruths and distortions until we are able to change our perceptions.

The skin uses sweat to regulate the internal temperature of the body. Truth also regulates the internal environment.

How do we obtain truth and how do we know when something is true? One way is through time. Time is a great purifier. We often have to let time and patience (the nutrient of the excretory system) do their work before we can see what is true and what is false. We can then use the barometer of truth to decide what is true for us.

If we find ourselves uncomfortable as a result of sweating or dealing with toxic elements in our lives, we might need to utilize some of the tools listed below to bring us back into balance with truth. When we see things in our skin that we don't want to see or when our skin feels uncomfortable, this is a message to us that we have an opportunity to realign with truth.

Alaskan Sweet Grass Flower Essence. In *The Essence of Healing (Second Edition)*, indications that this flower essence is needed are: inappropriate emotional attachment to others, emotional energies blocked in the lower chakras, and poor emotional communication with others (i.e., we are defensive, lack clarity, or our interactions are characterized by conflict, guilt, and the assignment of blame). Available from *www.alaskanessences.com*.

The Shake Hands–Crocus blend of essential oils is designed to give the body permission to enjoy peace, feel fulfilled, be optimistic, and shrug off burdens. The words "shake hands" indicate that this information has been accepted only after a struggle. The struggle consisted of feeling indecisive—as though there was no way out, as though there was no way to be except introverted and withdrawn. All of these situations are indicative of feeling worthless. Let's throw away that negative set of values and shake hands with our new way of being, which is being peaceful, feeling fulfilled, being optimistic and being able to shrug off burdens. This blend has been processed on the Terra Spun[ii] to give it an electrical charge, which in turn means that Shake Hands–Crocus affects your body's emotional field of information.

Ancient Forest Fairy Lantern Flower Essence.
Positive qualities: healthy maturation, acceptance of adult responsibilities. Patterns of imbalance: immaturity, helplessness, neediness, childish dependency, inability to shoulder responsibility. This flower essence is available from *www.essencesonline.com*.

Young Living's White Angelica Essential Oil Blend
"increases the aura around the body to bring in a delicate sense of strength and protection; this creates a feeling of wholeness in the realm of one's own spirituality. The frequency of the blend neutralizes negative energy and provides a feeling of protection and security." *Essential Oils Desk Reference (Third Edition)*, compiled by Essential Science Publishing

> *Truth is the health-giving nutrient of the Integumentary System.*

Skin/Reliability

Reliability means you can be counted on, depended on, and trusted. "He's reliable—he'll be here." "She's reliable—she'll get it done." If you're reliable, that means others can lean on you because they know you'll come through.

Our skin protects the vulnerable organs and glands inside our body. The skin is a buffer between our inside and outside world. The skin can take abuse and quickly repair itself. The skin stretches to accommodate our movement. The skin can sense a loving touch or pain. It is by definition sensitive and strong, which is the perfect description of reliability.

Immune System/Unity

Unity is an inner movement to create.

This creation can be a worthy movement…or it can be a disaster. Often it starts with one person and blossoms into a group whose members all move together to create a new reality. Creation can start with a cause and spread like wildfire from one person to another.

Our immune system creates in a similar way: it starts with one cell acknowledging the presence of something. That cell then passes on the information to many other cells.

When a cell is not allowed to acknowledge a foreign invasion, we call this "immune system suppression." Immune suppression is often a sought-after condition in medical procedures, particularly in the case of organ transplants. If the transplanted organ is detected by the immune system, it begins a process to reject the transplant because of the natural inclination of the immune system to protect the body.

Immune deficiency can also occur. This may happen when there is an insufficient response from the immune system. Contrary to immune suppression, immune deficiency is never desired as it allows pathogens harmful to the body to creep in unaware and undetected. Even if a pathogen is detected, the immune system may not have sufficient energy to mount a defense against it.

In order for the immune system to be successful, the whole body has to work together and contribute to the production of defense. The creation of a new state of being must also be supported. As we can see, the immune system is a complicated system that draws from many of the body's other systems. Health, then, is brought about by many components working together.

The movement to create requires action. If no action is taken by the immune system, the health of the body cannot be maintained—many organisms and pathogens are encountered every day and must be dealt with.

When we have disorder within our immune system, how can we nourish our being with the nutrient of unity to recreate our health?

We rely upon our definition of unity—a movement to create—to bring us to the first step.

First, we must move toward our goals and objectives. If we find ourselves making excuses to not move toward our goals even when we know that moving forward is in our best interests, we know we are dealing with the presence of fear. Creation can be halted by disorganization, fear of exposure, intimidation, strong opposition, and by many other things.

The things that we think of as blocking or stopping us are actually our teachers. They push and prod us to move forward in our creation process. Disorganization can drive us to create a new reality for ourselves, a reality wherein we discipline our movements and actions.

Fear of exposure can help us to work toward more confidence in our lives. We might join Toastmasters International or improve our appearance (wear new clothes, get a new hairdo, lose weight, etc.). Whatever it takes to build confidence will move us toward our goal of creating. Blockages and obstacles in our path to health can be likened to immune suppression.

Moving toward unity requires that we become aware. If we're aware of what's stopping our forward progress, we can begin to take steps to change what's holding us back. If we're unaware of our own challenges, there's little possibility for change. This lack of awareness can be likened to an immune deficiency in the body.

> "Many men go fishing all their lives without knowing it is not fish they are after." **Henry David Thoreau, 1817–1862.**

When we're unaware of what's occurring in our lives, it's easy to let a situation drag on and on. It's like turning a blind eye to a bunch of free-loaders eating all the food in your refrigerator and sleeping on your couch, throwing their clothes and belongings all over the house. You see it in your peripheral vision, but you don't want to say anything. Being half-asleep means you'll put up little or no objection to the invasion. Eventually, though, you'll have a crisis situation that seems to have come from out of the blue—except that it's actually been building and building because of a (perhaps deliberate) lack of awareness on your part.

When the immune system functions the way it should, foreign pathogens are engulfed by the cells; the cells then digest the pathogens. Energy can't be destroyed, however, so the correct way to understand this situation is that the energy of the pathogen has been transformed. Through inclusion (or engulfment or digestion), this transformation takes the old energy and uses it to create a whole new state of being. This is the role of a healthy, fully functioning immune system.

When we become aware of and focus on (surround) something in our lives—whether it's disorganization or fear of exposure or intimidation—this awareness can alter our reality. We can decide to change our lives by giving energy and action to whatever has been blocking our path. In truth, nothing actually goes away; rather, it's transformed into a new way of being. Disorganization becomes organization. Intimidation becomes confidence. The things we needed to organize didn't vanish, but we can begin to treat the disorganized things in a completely new way. Transforming disorganization into organization frees us to continue on the path to creation. If we let the disorganization (or the intimidation or the fear) stop us, however, our new way of being and/or progress toward our goal is stalled, meaning we can't step onto our new path.

In summarizing this information, we can see how unity is an inner movement to create. The allowance of creation requires awareness, agreement, and action. We need to take action to transform the invaders. We need to know that energy cannot be destroyed, but rather changed into something that is no longer a threat. We need to see how blockades in our lives can be teachers. These teachers are pointing and directing, pushing and prodding us to make changes that can transform our negative inner aspects into positive inner aspects. These changes can then lead to the ultimate creation of health and wholeness.

Unity is a movement to create. The creation we are moving toward is health. The steps in the movement toward creation are:

Becoming aware.

Being in agreement.

Taking action.

And appreciating our obstacles as being our teachers; these teachers guide us toward creating health.

The following list of tools may help us move toward awareness so that we can address the things in our lives that require transformation. Only then can we create health.

Sapphire gemstones from Love is in the Earth by Melody: "The sapphire is known as a stone of prosperity; it sustains the gifts of life by eliminating frustration and fulfilling the dreams and desires of the consciousness. Sapphires tend to focus, emanate, and radiate energy without conscious initiation." To increase the vibration and power of the sapphire gemstones, increase their mass. Gemstones are available in gem and rock shops throughout the United States or you can find them online.

Properties of <u>Chrysoprase gemstones</u> are "Cooling properties—it's used for healing in various ways (i.e., in burns and neck strain). Chrysoprase gemstones are believed to release negativity from the body and to heal a broken heart. This gentle and soothing gemstone is often known as one that brings happiness, peace, and tolerance to its wearer; it expels anger, negative thoughts, and irritability. Chrysoprase is friendly and provides spiritual protection. It also prevents depression and acts as a shield against any incoming negativity. It strengthens the reproductive organs—the ovaries, testicles, fallopian tubes, and prostate—and increases fertility and opens the sexual chakra. Chrysoprase often brings good fortune and prosperity; this stone is considered a good luck stone. Because of its color, Chrysoprase gemstone is also related to money and success." (From *www.indianetzone.com.*)

Desert Broom Flower Essence. "When we want to accomplish something but all parts of our being are not in alignment with our desire, desert broom helps us to find resolution and readiness to take the next step. Resolution is the key word for this essence, especially when we want to go deeply into a matter but there is something holding us back. Harmonizing Qualities: centered, gathered together, unified; helping to bring a definite resolution, to attain the state of readiness needed to take the next step. Patterns of imbalance: a kind of apathy (seeing all of the possibilities and not seeing a single strong way OR seeing only the strong way and not all of the possibilities), something standing in the way of your desire to delve into a matter (wanting to do something, yet all facets of you are not lining up behind that desire)." From *The Alchemy of the Desert (Second Edition)*. Please refer to this book for in-depth information about this flower essence. (This flower essence is available from *www.desert-alchemy.com*.)

Magnet Therapy. Generally speaking, the South Pole of a magnet encourages the proliferation of things needing to undergo a transformation. If you are harboring a pathogen such as a bacteria or a virus, you would NOT want to use the South Pole of a magnet—this will encourage the profusion of the foreign invader. The North Pole of a magnet suppresses proliferation; in this case, it will halt the growth of the foreign invasion. In *The Body Magnetic* by Buryl Payne, Ph.D. (Sixth Edition, 1996), he lists specific body ailments that may be eased by the application of magnet therapy. He also strongly cautions us NOT to use South Pole magnets on tumors, cancers, or infections as this encourages the growth of the bacteria or virus that might be present.

> *Unity is the health-giving nutrient of the Immune System.*

Section 2

Quick Reference Guide to Systems, Organs, Glands

Systems:
- **Cardiovascular System** — **Joy**
- **Digestive System** — **Temperance**
- **Endocrine System** — **Peace**
- **Excretory System** — **Patience**
- **Immune System** — **Unity**
- **Integumentary System** — **Truth**
- **Lymphatic System** — **Forgiveness**
- **Muscular System** — **Teachable**
- **Nervous System** — **Gentleness**
- **Respiratory System** — **Love**
- **Reproductive System** — **Faith**
- **Skeletal System** — **Quality**

Organs:
- **Bladder** — **Uplifted**
- **Brain** — **Justice**
- **Colon** — **Authenticity**
- **Heart** — **Meaning**
- **Kidneys** — **(Consistent and Coherent)**

Assurance
Liver	**Stability**
Lungs	**Kindness**
Skin	**Reliability**
Small Intestine	**Highly Valued**
Stomach	**Strength**
Uterus	**Consciousness**

Glands:
Adrenals	**Sensibility**
Ovaries	**Optimism**
Pancreas	**(Unconquerable) Loyalty**
Prostate	**Invigorated & Productive**
Testes	**Self-Esteem**
Thyroid	**Certainty**

Other:
Blood	**Making Progress**

Quick Product Reference

Cardiovascular System/Joy
- Joy Mandala
- Joy Savory
- Joy Tactile
- Joy Triz
- Amethyst Gemstones
- Color Yellow
- Roses, Daffodils, Tulips

Digestive System/Temperance
- Affirmations
- Temperance Wisdom Sachet
- Citrine, Topaz, Tourmaline, Tanzanite, Amethyst Gemstone combination
- Shake Hands–Crocus

Endocrine System/Peace
- Peace Mandala
- Sun Planetary Tuning Fork
- Peace Wisdom Sachet
- Ruby Gem Elixir

Excretory System/Patience
- Dancing
- Sapphires, Moonstones, Onyx combined
- Patience Triz
- Patience Wisdom Sachet

Integumentary System/Truth
- Sweet Grass Flower Essence
- Fairy Lantern Flower Essence
- Shake Hands–Crocus
- White Angelica Young Living Essential Oil Blend

Immune System/Unity
- Sapphire Gemstones
- Chrysoprase Gemstones
- Desert Broom Flower Essences
- Magnets

Lymphatic System/Forgiveness
- Quartz Crystals
- Forgiveness Triz
- Shake Hands–Daffodil
- Touch

Muscular System/Teachable
- Royal Blue Pomander
- Teachable Mandala
- Teachable Savory
- Dandelion Flower Essence

QUICK PRODUCT REFERENCE

Nervous System/Gentleness
- **Rabbit Moiety**
- **Gentle Cell**
- **Amazonite and Sapphire Gemstones**
- **Skin Brushing**

Reproductive System/Faith
- **Faith Mandala**
- **Faith Triz**
- **Pearl Gem Elixir**
- **Petrified Forest Flower Essence**

Respiratory System/Love
- **Affirmations**
- **Love Mandala**
- **Sage Flower Essence**
- **Gentle Baby Young Living Essential Oil Blend**

Skeletal System/Quality
- **Essential Oils of Basil, Frankincense, and Valerian combined**
- **Diamond Gem Elixir**
- **Quality Savory**
- **Quality Tactile**
- **Quality Triz**
- **Poppies, Apple Blossoms, Indian Paintbrush**

Healing Words

"When you can transcend your malaise and thoughts of impossible or incurable, and replace them with the energy of spirit where all things are possible, the material world responds and wholeness replaces visions of doom and separateness. Deliver this higher energy thinking to even the worst of circumstances and a spiritual solution is revealed." Wayne W. Dyer, There's a Spiritual Solution to every problem.

As a society we have been taught that what we ingest is what gives us energy. Words also, when ingested and brought into our innermost being, provide powerful energy as well. Words are an expression of your intentions. If you listen to the words you speak you will see more of your own heart. Becoming conscious is one of the first steps we take toward using our words as an instrument.

Words are one of the best, most powerful, healing tools we can grasp and utilize. Words can uplift and they can devastate. Words are at the vibratory level of the angels and guides. They carry nutrition much like food and water. According to the gurus of today, your future can be spoken into existence. If your future can be wrapped up in words, you see the wisdom in choosing them carefully.

The following words are nutritious words—their vibrations match the vibrations of the organ, gland, problem, or system that is mentioned. These words can be used as affirmations. One set of the given words is equal to one "dose." **You'll notice that some of the words are repeated within each set. This is not a misprint, but rather the formula for that vibration.** Therefore, if you want a stronger vibration, you will need to repeat the sets of the words more often.

These words can also be used to pray for someone else; your intention can direct the energy flow. Singing the words also adds another dimension to the healing, as does writing or journaling the words. They do not have to make sense to you right away—as you work with them, you will begin to see patterns within yourself. You will see that you can benefit by changing your internal perception and beliefs about yourself.

You can also pray, say, write, or sing the words without making them into statements. As you say them, ponder their meaning and reflect upon how they pertain to you.

If you are using the words to pray for someone else, change the wording to reflect this—i.e., YOU are authentic, YOUR life is plausible, etc.

(These sample affirmations use the nutrient package of the colon.)

I am authentic. My life is plausible. I am the real stuff. I am genuine. I am the real stuff. I am the real McCoy. I am the real stuff. My life is legitimate and genuine. I am credible and valid, the real McCoy. My life is genuine and credible. I am believable and credible.

The list of healing words, formatted so you can print them on business size cards, is available on the website www.burdickinstitute.com.

Assurance which is coherent and consistent (kidneys)

Authority, sureness, safety net, self-confidence, certainty, self-assurance, dedication, affirmation, guarantee, oath, promise, vow, sureness, confidence, certainty, sureness, self-confidence, sure, affirmation, sureness, guarantee, profession, sureness, confidence, sureness

Authenticity (Colon)

Plausibility, real stuff, genuineness, real stuff, real McCoy, real stuff, legitimacy, genuine, credible, valid, real McCoy, genuineness, real stuff, genuineness, credible, believable, credible

Certainty (Thyroid)

Certain, positive, marked certainty, sureness, noted certainty, wholly convinced, total certainty, sureness, indisputable, marked certainty, assured, noted certainty

Consciousness (Uterus)

Insight, self-knowledge, appreciation, understanding, foresight, knowing, foresight, knowing, appreciation, comprehension, alive, conscious, self-awareness

Faith (Reproductive System)

Faith, conviction, trust, conviction, belief, commit, conviction, hope, expectancy, promise, conviction, expectancy, anticipation, go for it, conviction, anticipation

Forgiveness (Lymphatic System)

Forgiveness, mercy, mercifulness, pardon, mercifulness, mercy, mercifulness, pardon, mercifulness, mercy, mercy, pardon, mercy, pardon, mercy, mercifulness, pardon, mercy

Gentleness (Nervous System)

Conduct, gentleness, good manners, gentleness, presence, conduct, presence, manner

Highly Valued (Small Intestines)

Semiprecious, priceless, valued, sacred, expensive, worth, rich, priceless, worthy, invaluable, important, expensive, priceless, valued, semiprecious

Invigorated (Prostate) – also see productive

Spirited, lively, life, effervescent, peppy, refreshed, rested, spirited, effusive, energetic, effervescent, effusive, effervescent, energetic, alive, alert, energetic, effervescent, energetic

Joy (Cardiovascular System)

Rejoice, delight, gladden, joyfulness, joyousness, gladden, delight, gladden, joyousness, delight, gladden, gladden, gladden, gladden delight, gladden, delight, delight

Justice (Brain)

Equity moderation, prudent, fortitude, justness, just, moderation, temperance, fairness, fortitude, moderation, prudent, rightfulness, moderation, prudent

Love (Respiratory System)

Emotion, passion ,create love, emotion, love life, love, passion, create love, emotion, passion, love, passion, emotion, love life, passion, passion, create love, passion, passion, passion, create love, passion, passion

Loyalty (Pancreas)

Caring, devotion cooperation, commitment, allegiance, faithful, consecration, loyal, caring, faith, allegiance, faithful, faith, allegiance

Making Progress (Blood)

March on, procession, onward motion, movement, march, procession

Meaning (Heart)

Resolute, purposive, purposeful, meaningful, significant, important, resolute, earnest, substantive, purposeful, significant, purposeful, remarkable, noteworthy, important

Optimism (Ovaries)

Hopeful, feeling, cheerfulness, friendly, spirited, willing, optimistic, hope, encouraged, friendly, hope, hopeful, hope, encouraged

Peace (Endocrine System)

Order, harmony, concord, harmony, ataraxis, order, concordance, harmony, repose, order, harmony, concord, pacification, harmony, order

Patience (Excretory System)

Longanimity, patience, forbear, holdup, longanimity, delay, longanimity, grace, forbearance, forbear, patience, good nature, longanimity, delay, holdup, patience, patience, patience, holdup, patience

Productive (Prostate) – also see invigorated

Creative, profitable, originative, original, rich, generative, creative, creative, fat, creative, originative, fat, originative, generative, original, original, generative

Quality (Skeletal System)

Attribute, prize, positive, good, positive, prize, positive, attribute, positive, caliber, good, prime, choice, positive, good, caliber

Reliability (Skin)

Dependable, duplicability, responsible, dependable, responsible, integrity, responsible, dependability, integrity, responsibility, trustworthy

Self-Esteem (Testes)

Self-love, self-importance, self-esteem, pride, respect, admiration, honor, prize, approval, appreciation, self-importance, respect, admiration, appreciate, honor

Sensibility (Adrenals)

Awareness, sentience, awareness, hypersensitivity, sensitiveness, sensation, stream of consciousness, responsiveness, sense, hypersensitivity, responsiveness, waking, aware, consciousness, perceive, discernment, wisdom, prudence, discernment, perceive

Stability (Liver)

Tranquility, order, firmness, order, steadiness, quiet, firmness, constancy, constancy, constant, stability, harmony, stability, concord, order

Strength (Stomach)

Strong, powerful, strong, robust, iron-like, rugged, potent, brawny, potent, compelling, tough, strong, sturdy, robust, stalwart, strength, powerful, iron-like, tough

Teachable (Muscular System)

Learn, educate, enlighten, suggest, cultivate, improve, alter, modify, enhance, propose, show, recommend, report, teach, communicate

Temperance (Digestive System)

Prudence, temperance, worth, prize, appreciate, acknowledge, moderation, merit, valuable, choice, decide, settle, determine, concord, agree, evidenced
Truth (Integumentary System)

Truth (Integumentary System)

Verity, true, actual, sincere, faithful, right, sure, true, factual actual, truthful, honorable, actual, honest, indisputable, assured, actual

Unity (Immune System)

One, whole, single, same, unit, peerless, incomparable, unparalleled, peerless, similar, uniform, unity, peerless, unique, extraordinary, peerless, uniform, complete, same, unit, complete, unique

Uplifted (Bladder)

Elated, jubilant, triumphant, suspended, buttressed, braced, backed up, supported, fostered, bond, hold, truss, triumphant, fostered, triumphant

Gemstones, short and sweet

Gemstones, like all of nature, have their own special vibration creating their own unique message. This list is very short and sweet, getting right to the point of explaining their vibration in concise terms. This list can be expounded upon with many, many words, but we have found that it is helpful to keep it simple. This way we can remember the major vibration of each stone and understand how the message applies to our own lives. The impacts mentioned in the third column represent the biggest impact the gemstone has on the body. Of course, the gemstones also influence other organs, glands, and systems, but the impression is not as strong as the one listed in this column.

Gemstone	*Nutrient*	*Impacts*
Agates	wisdom	meaning/heart
Amazonite	dignity	kindness/lungs
Amethyst	joyful	joy/cardiovascular system
Aquamarine	merciful	kindness/lungs
Bloodstone	refreshed	reliability/skin

Chrysoprase	steadfast	highly valued/small intestines
Citrine	embracing truth	assurance/kidneys
Diamond	organized	love/respiratory system
Emerald	compassion	forgiveness/lymphatic sys.
Fluorite	simplicity	certainty/thyroid
Garnet	honored (as opposed to compromised)	stability/liver
Hematite	released	strength/stomach
Moonstone	outgoing	consciousness/uterus
Onyx	skillful	sensibility/adrenals
Opal	strong	unity/immune system
Peridot	unbiased, fresh perspective	loyalty/pancreas
Quartz crystals	forgiveness	forgiveness/lymphatic system
Rhodochrosite	concentration	quality/skeletal system
Ruby	accountable	stability/liver
Sapphire	powerful	teachable/muscular system
Tanzanite	resolute	gentleness/nervous system
Topaz	growing (not in a rut)	loyalty/pancreas
Tourmaline	looking forward	authenticity/colon
Turquoise	curable	faith/reproductive system

The Emotional Language of Essential Oils

Essential oils are very concentrated vibrational substances. They convey the message of the plant or tree that they are extracted from. They can be combined to create a more paragraph type of message or they can be used alone. The combining of essential oils is an art that requires sensitivity on the part of the formulator. D. Gary Young, N.D., from Young Living Essential Oils taught the importance of knowing how to combine the essential oils to obtain the results you are seeking.

Since essential oils are concentrated, a single drop can send a powerful message to the body. Most people study essential oils for their chemical constituents, which is a very exacting science and beyond the scope of this book. We have found that by knowing the emotional action of the oil combined with the knowledge of the emotional component of the organs, glands, and systems, you can effectively correlate this information and help yourself.

The following lists give information on the single essential oils that are available. We use Young Living essential oils exclusively because we are confident and assured of the purity of the essential oils. There are other good companies that sell essential oils, but we are not familiar with them; therefore, we cannot recommend them. Just be aware that chemicals can be added to essential oils that are undetectable by smell, and if they have been adulterated by chemicals, the essential oil will not be able to produce the expected results.

The first list (<u>The Essential Oil Profile</u>) of the essential oil messages displays the essential oil with the positive + information, along with information on the disbursement of negative information and the areas that will have a direct impact from the essential oil.

The second list (<u>The Essential Oil Nutrients</u>) displays the body's nutrients and the appropriate essential oils that supply these nutrients.

The third list (<u>The Essential Oil Positive States</u>) allows you to look for the positive emotion you might be seeking cross-referenced with the list of the essential oil that supplies that emotional message.

And the fourth list (<u>The Essential Oil vs. Negative States</u>) compiles the negative emotions that may be dispelled by the use of the essential oil. This gives you more than one way to find information. At times we can only identify with the negative emotion we are feeling. Once you find the negative aspect you are feeling, you can then compare this to the positive emotion listed for that essential oil to see what you need to be feeding yourself for the sense of well-being that you seek.

For example, our first essential oil, Basil, has a positive message that says to the body "included, approval, submissive, bearable, supported, settled, and confident." These positive messages disburse the emotions of defeat and agitation, division, feeling flawed and inadequate. This information will have a direct impact on the state of being teachable (muscular system), stable (liver), invigorated, and productive (prostate).

You could understand this information as follows, using this formula for each essential oil:

I now am _teachable_, for I am included, approved of, and able to be submissive. I am now teachable for I am supported, things are bearable, and I am settled and confident. (Affecting muscular system)
I now am _stable,_ for I am included, approved of, and able to be submissive. I am now stable for I am supported, things are bearable. I am settled and confident. (Affecting liver)
I now am _invigorated and productive,_ for I am included, approved of, able to be submissive. I am now invigorated and productive, for I am supported, things are bearable. I am settled and confident. (Affecting prostate)

For more information on the Direct Impact, please refer to the chapters on the particular emotions, or to the quick reference pages.

The Essential Oil Profile List

"You can live a life of fear or live a life of love. You have the choice! But I can tell you that if you choose to see a world of love, your body will respond by growing in health. If you choose to believe that you live in a dark world full of fear, your body's health will be compromised as you physiologically close yourself down in a protection response." *The Biology of Belief,* Bruce Lipton Ph.D.

SINGLE ESSENTIAL OILS

Basil
+message: Included, approval, submissive, bearable, supported, settled, confident
Disburses: defeat, agitation, division, feeling flawed and inadequate
Direct Impact: teachable, stability, invigorated, and productive

Bergamot
+message: wise, confident, self-esteem
Disburses: know-it-all, unprepared
Direct Impact: unity, sensibility

Cedarwood
+message: kind, peaceful, motivated, comforted
Disburses: lack of peace, punished, unbearable
Direct Impact: kindness, loyalty, temperance

Cedar, Red Canadian
+message: selfless, efficient, confidence, virtue
Disburses: cruelty
Direct Impact: kindness, joy

Chamomile, Roman
+message: plenty of room, finished, comforted
Disburses: melancholy, unresolved issues
Direct Impact: stability, temperance

Cinnamon Bark
+message: life works for me, exceptional, grateful, motivated
Disburses: pettiness, suicidal, unsure
Direct Impact: authenticity, inspiration (eyes)

Cistus
+message: blissful, I feel sensitive, total forgiveness, loved
Disburses: struggling, unlovable, vulnerability
Direct Impact: kindness, unity, love

Clary Sage
+message: accepted, favored, supported, renewed
Disburses: boxed in, discredited, ticked off
Direct Impact: kindness, faith

Clove
+message: praised, peace of mind, peace, valued, strong
Disburses: fatigue, ruination, shock, weakness
Direct Impact: stability, kindness, peace

Coriander
+message: invigorated, trust, responsive, brightened
Disburses: insecurity, repelling others, unappreciated
Direct Impact: trust, invigorated, progressing, making progress

Cypress
+message: liberated, chaste, graceful, steadfast
Disburses: feeling of abandonment, thwarted, persecuted
Direct Impact: stability, forgiveness

Dill
+message: assured, decent
Disburses: neglect, feeling needy, unworthy
Direct Impact: temperance, value

Elemi
+message: resolute, sure, steadfast
Disburses: frustrated, feeling alone, defeated, hostile
Direct Impact: stability, certainty, confidence (inner ears)

Eucalyptus Globilus
+message: peace, worthy, agreeable, loving
Disburses: feeling ridiculous, lonely, jealous, indecent
Direct Impact: peace, kindness, love, temperance

Eucalyptus Polybrachtea
+message: agreeable, forgiveness, assurance
Disburses: discredited, goofed up, mortified
Direct Impact: truth, sensibility, assurance, forgiveness

Fennel
+message: respect, peaceful, acclaimed, powerful
Disburses: competitive, disruptive
Direct Impact: kindness, sensibility, temperance, valued, unity

Fir (Abies alba)
+message: pardoned, forgiven, concerned, caring
Disburses: emotional stress, unfeeling, don't care
Direct Impact: kindness, sensibility, loyalty, joy, temperance, faith

Fir (white)
+message: safe
Disburses: suspicion
Direct Impact: meaning, certainty, authenticity

Frankincense
+message: unconditional forgiveness, stability,
Disburses: disapproval, inconsistency
Direct Impact: sensibility, joy, kindness, love, unity

Galbanum
+message: cherished, tolerance, careful, virtuous, admirable
Disburses: cheated, exhaustion, impassive, selfish
Direct Impact: gentleness, peace, certainty, forgiveness

Geranium
+message: confident, accepted, faith in self and God, stable, caring peace, provided for
Disburses: accused, banished, chronic anxiety, longing, need (have to) protect self
Direct Impact: justice, assurance, certainty, joy

Ginger
+message: responsive, joy, joyful, strong, competent
Disburses: grief, quitting unqualified
Direct Impact: reliable, meaning, strength, optimism, forgiveness

Goldenrod
+message: good, unrestrained, stable, admirable
Disburses: dirty, enslaved, insanity, need for approval, shameful
Direct Impact: reliable, kindness, teachable, patience, unity

Grapefruit
+message: accepted, valued, trustworthy, peaceful, mindful
Disburses: banished, imposter, repressed, thoughtlessness
Direct Impact: justice, kindness, authenticity, uplifted, certainty, loyalty, forgiveness

Helichrysum
+message: happy, loving, and serene
Disburses: agitated, closed off, intolerant, lack of opportunity, shoved aside, upset
Direct Impact: reliability, stability, highly valued, uplifted, loyalty, teachable, peace, forgiveness, truth

Hyssop
+message: invigorated, exuberant, unconditional love, demonstrates love easily, pleasant
Disburses: beaten down, driven, grudges, lack of affection, repulsed by others
Direct Impact: reliable, meaning, assurance, consciousness, joy, forgiveness, faith

Jasmine
+message: welcomed, acceptance, you are acknowledged, serene, loving, and winsome
Disburses: banished, disapproval, ignored, nervous, self-centered, unloved
Direct Impact: kindness, loyalty, quality, forgiveness, unity

Juniper
+message: tenacious, undefeated
Disburses: defeated, vengeance
Direct Impact: kindness, stability, assurance, certainty, quality, forgiveness, faith

Laurus Nobilis
+message: accepts truth, balanced, peace
Disburses: repression, unjust
Direct Impact: kindness, uplifted, teachable, peace, love

Lavender
+message: happy, delighted, total forgiveness, vibrant
Disburses: discord
Direct Impact: reliability, kindness, assurance, strength, teachable, joy, temperance, unity

Ledum
+ message: mercy, calm, full of faith
Disburses: boiling inside, grieved, lack of support, reprobate
Direct Impact: reliability, stability, highly valued, uplifted, certainty, edified, teachable, love, unity

Lemon
+message: respectful, valiant
Disburses: bragging, fearful, feeling like scum, useless
Direct Impact: reliability, stability, consciousness, certainty, loyalty, quality, patience

Lemongrass
+message: assertive, cherished
Disburses: alienated, clingy, hesitant, neglected, uncomfortable, unmindful
Direct Impact: justice, stability, strength, certainty, loyalty, gentleness, patience, temperance

Marjoram
+message: honored, courageous, calm, reverent
Disburses: compromised, disheartened, driven, unkind
Direct Impact: reliability, meaning, assurance, uplifted, peace, joy, forgiveness

Melaleuca Alternifolia
+message: cheerful, calm, looking forward
Disburses: belligerent, discordant, irked, reticent
Direct Impact: quality, patience, unity, kindness, assurance, uplifted

Melaleuca Ericifolia
+message: good luck, passionate
Disburses: bad luck, frigid, restless, self-consciousness, weariness
Direct Impact: peace, love, unity, kindness, uplifted, self-esteem, loyalty

Mountain Savory
+message: supreme joy, affable
Disburses: bashful, lack of courage, obnoxious, slave (feeling like a)

Direct Impact: gentleness, love, faith, stability, authenticity, uplifted

<u>Myrrh</u>

+message: cheerful, healthy, unconditional love
Disburses: belligerent, dreadful, livid, rushed, violated
Direct Impact: gentleness, joy, strength, invigorated, productive, and optimistic

<u>Myrtle</u>

+message: accepted, released, contentment
Disburses: banished, entangled, lost, strife
Direct Impact: quality, peace, temperance, kindness, stability, authenticity, consciousness, self-esteem, certainty, edified

<u>Nutmeg</u>

+message: forgiveness, acceptance, peace, considerate
Disburses: anguish, drowning (like I'm), self-condemnation
Direct Impact: joy, forgiveness, faith, kindness, meaning, assurance

<u>Orange</u>

+message: pleasant, relaxed
Disburses: pushed, unkindness
Direct Impact: quality, peace, joy, reliability, meaning, assurance, strength, loyalty

Oregano
+message: honest, I am decisive
Disburses: betrayal, resentment
Direct Impact: teachable, peace, temperance, kindness, stability, highly valued, uplifted, loyalty

Patchouli
+message: gregarious, mellow, caring
Disburses: over-sensitive, quitting, tempted
Direct Impact: quality, joy, unity, kindness, authenticity, uplifted, loyalty

Pepper, Black
+message: comfortable, serene, and peaceful
Disburses: enslaved, grief, morbid, ugly
Direct Impact: quality, patience, forgiveness, unity, kindness, stability, authenticity, uplifted, loyalty

Peppermint
+message: accepting, benevolence, looking forward to, thoughtful
Disburses: competitive, murmuring, overworked
Direct Impact: quality, patience, temperance, assurance, loyalty

Petitgrain
+message: humble, good, responsible, kind
Disburses: animosity, enraged, joyless, shocked
Direct Impact: quality, love, unity, reliable, kindness, stability, uplifted, self-esteem

Pine
   +message: in tune with, feeling and centered
   Disburses: anger, enraged, feeling poor
   Direct Impact: peace, love, unity, reliable, meaning, assurance, uplifted

Ravensara
   +message: peaceful, remembered, fulfillment, caring, flowing
   Disburses: boxed in, distraught, empty, shunned
   Direct Impact: forgiveness, kindness, authenticity, self-esteem, edified

Rose
   +message: supreme joy, sought after, focused
   Disburses: feeling old, fierce, neurotic attachments, weariness
   Direct Impact: patience, forgiveness, reliable, meaning, assurance,

Rosemary
   +message: determined, adaptable
   Disburses: luckless, stagnant
   Direct Impact: quality, joy, unity, kindness, stability, certainty

Rosemary Verbenon
   +message: acknowledged, disciplined
   Disburses: feeling ridiculous, powerless
   Direct Impact: quality, joy, unity, reliable, meaning, assurance, certainty

Rosewood
+message: connected, flexible
Disburses: lying, hopeless
Direct Impact: teachable, joy, forgiveness, unity, reliable, meaning, assurance, uplifted, optimism

Sage
+message: included, renewed
Disburses: lack of self-confidence, used
Direct Impact: quality, peace, joy, forgiveness, faith, kindness, authenticity, uplifted, certainty

Sandalwood
+message: care about self, appreciated, powerful
Disburses: self-contempt, useless
Direct Impact: teachable, peace, forgiveness, assurance, invigorated and productive, optimism

Spikenard
+message: aligned, wise, uplifted
Disburses: immobilized, longing, tribulation
Direct Impact: joy, temperance, meaning, assurance, strength, sensibility

Spruce
+message: yielding, proficient, teachable
Disburses: obsessed, slothful, and unloved
Direct Impact: teachable, joy, forgiveness, unity, kindness, stability, certainty

Spearmint
+message: unconditional love, commended, unselfish
Disburses: fainthearted, luckless, I'm not enough
Direct Impact: teachable, peace, temperance, reliable, meaning, authentic, and uplifted

Tangerine
+message: enthused, directed, invigorated
Disburses: friendless, repulsive
Direct Impact: gentleness, patience, reliable, meaning, assurance, strength, certainty

Tansy, Idaho
+message: indispensable, attended to, pampered
Disburses: forlorn, martyr, sinking feeling
Direct Impact: teachable, gentleness, unity, stability, certainty, loyalty

Tarragon
+message: moving forward, liberated, radiant
Disburses: naïve, obstinate, victimization
Direct Impact: patience, love, temperance, assurance

Thyme
+message: free of burdens, steadfast, accepts self, regarded highly, refreshed
Disburses: devalued, evil-minded, stressed, and violated
Direct Impact: Forgiveness, unity, kindness, assurance, and certainty

Thyme, Linalol
+message: coordinated, forgiveness, considerate
Disburses: lack of courage, nervous, resistant
Direct Impact: joy, temperance, kindness, stability, authenticity, certainty

Tsuga
+message: accepting, covered, I'm enough, reasonable
Disburses: boiling inside, failing, naughty, suppressed, always wrong
Direct Impact: joy, stability, loyalty

Valerian
+message: authentic, taken care of, dignified, lovable
Disburses: belief in being degenerative, enraged, needs approval, talks too much
Direct Impact: forgiveness, kindness, highly-valued, edified, loyalty, optimism, invigorated and productive

Vetiver
+message: upright, comprehending, open-minded, motivated
Disburses: boisterous, deceit, can't face up to issues, restless
Direct Impact: gentleness, patience, forgiveness, kindness, stability, assurance

Vitex
+messages: capable, progressing
Disburses: (feeling like) a slave, mixed up

Direct Impact: forgiveness, kindness, sensibility

<u>Wintergreen</u>
 +message: capable, cooperative
 Disburses: ineffective, I'm not enough
 Direct Impact: teachable, quality, peace, meaning, uplifted

<u>Ylang-Ylang</u>
 +message: accelerated, progressive
 Disburses: I'm nothing
 Direct Impact: peace, forgiveness, faith, reliable, meaning, authenticity

The Essential Oil Nutrient List

"...specific healing and balancing patterns that are vital to humans have been incorporated in the makeup of plant life." Machaelle Small Wright, *Flower Essences,* page 3

<u>Assurance, nutrient of the kidneys</u>
- **Eucalyptus Polybrachtea**
- **Geranium**
- **Hyssop**
- **Juniper**
- **Lavender**
- **Marjoram**
- **Melaleuca Alternifolia**
- **Nutmeg**
- **Orange**
- **Peppermint**
- **Pine**
- **Rose**
- **Rosemary Verbenon**
- **Rosewood**
- **Sandalwood**
- **Spikenard**

Tangerine
Tarragon
Thyme
Vetiver

Authenticity, nutrient of the colon
Cinnamon bark
Fir (white)
Grapefruit
Mountain Savory
Myrtle
Patchouli
Pepper, black
Ravensara
Sage
Spearmint
Thyme, Linalol
Ylang-Ylang

Certainty, nutrient of the thyroid
Elemi
Fir (white)
Galbanum
Geranium
Grapefruit
Juniper
Ledum
Lemon
Lemongrass
Myrtle
Rosemary
Rosemary Verbenon

Sage
Spruce
Tangerine
Tansy, Idaho
Thyme
Thyme, Linalol

Consciousness, nutrient of the uterus
Hyssop
Lemon
Myrtle

Faith, nutrient of the Reproductive System
Clary Sage
Coriander
Fir (Abies alba)
Hyssop
Juniper
Mountain Savory
Nutmeg
Sage
Ylang-Ylang

Forgiveness, nutrient of the Lymphatic System
Cypress
Eucalyptus Polybrachtea
Galbanum
Ginger
Grapefruit
Helichrysum
Hyssop
Jasmine

Juniper
Marjoram
Nutmeg
Pepper, Black
Ravensara
Rose
Rosewood
Sage
Sandalwood
Spruce
Thyme
Valerian
Vetiver
Vitex
Ylang-Ylang

Gentleness, nutrient of the Nervous System
Galbanum
Lemongrass
Mountain Savory
Myrrh
Tangerine
Tansy, Idaho
Vetiver

Highly Valued, nutrient of the Small Intestines
Helichrysum
Ledum
Oregano
Valerian

Invigorated and Productive, nutrient of the Prostate
- Basil
- Coriander
- Myrrh
- Sandalwood
- Valerian

Joy, nutrient of the Cardiovascular System
- Cedar, Red Canadian
- Fir (Abies alba)
- Frankincense
- Geranium
- Hyssop
- Lavender
- Marjoram
- Myrrh
- Nutmeg
- Orange
- Patchouli
- Rosemary
- Rosemary Verbenon
- Rosewood
- Sage
- Spikenard
- Spruce
- Thyme, Linalol
- Tsuga

Justice, nutrient of the brain
- Geranium
- Grapefruit
- Lemongrass

Love, nutrient of the Respiratory System
Cistus
Eucalyptus Globilus
Frankincense
Laurus Nobilis
Ledum
Melaleuca Ericifolia
Mountain Savory
Petitgrain
Pine
Tarragon

Loyalty, nutrient of the pancreas
Cedarwood
Fir (Abies alba)
Grapefruit
Helichrysum
Jasmine
Lemon
Lemongrass
Melaleuca Ericifolia
Orange
Oregano
Patchouli
Pepper, Black
Peppermint
Tansy, Idaho
Tsuga
Valerian

Kindness, nutrient of the lungs
- Cedarwood
- Cedar, Red Canadian
- Cistus
- Clary Sage
- Clove
- Eucalyptus Globulus
- Fennel
- Fir (Abies alba)
- Frankincense
- Goldenrod
- Grapefruit
- Jasmine
- Juniper
- Laurus Nobilis
- Lavender
- Melaleuca Alternifolia
- Melaleuca Ericifolia
- Myrtle
- Nutmeg
- Oregano
- Patchouli
- Pepper, Black
- Petitgrain
- Ravensara
- Rosemary
- Sage
- Spruce
- Thyme
- Thyme, Linalol

Valerian
Vetiver
Vitex

Making Progress, nutrient of the blood
Coriander

Meaning, nutrient of the heart
Fir, white
Ginger
Hyssop
Marjoram
Nutmeg
Orange
Pine
Rose
Rosemary Verbenon
Rosewood
Spikenard
Spearmint
Tangerine
Wintergreen
Ylang-Ylang

Optimism, nutrient of the ovaries
Ginger
Myrrh
Rosewood
Sandalwood
Valerian

Patience, nutrient of the Excretory System
- Goldenrod
- Lemon
- Lemongrass
- Melaleuca Alternifolia
- Pepper, Black
- Peppermint
- Rose
- Tangerine
- Tarragon
- Vetiver

Peace, nutrient of the Endocrine System
- Clove
- Eucalyptus Globilus
- Galbanum
- Helichrysum
- Laurus Nobilis
- Marjoram
- Melaleuca Ericifolia
- Myrtle
- Orange
- Oregano
- Pine
- Sage
- Sandalwood
- Spearmint
- Wintergreen
- Ylang-Ylang

Quality, nutrient of the Skeletal System
Jasmine
Juniper
Lemon
Melaleuca Alternifolia
Myrtle
Orange
Patchouli
Pepper, Black
Peppermint
Petitgrain
Rosemary
Rosemary Verbenon
Sage
Wintergreen

Reliability, nutrient of the skin
Ginger
Goldenrod
Helichrysum
Hyssop
Lavender
Ledum
Lemon
Marjoram
Orange
Petitgrain
Pine
Rose
Rosemary Verbenon
Rosewood
Spearmint

    Tangerine
    Ylang-Ylang

Self-Esteem, nutrient of the testes
    Melaleuca Ericifolia
    Myrtle
    Petitgrain
    Ravensara

Sensibility, nutrient of the adrenals
    Bergamot
    Eucalyptus Polybrachtea
    Fennel
    Fir (Abies alba)
    Frankincense
    Vitex

Stability, nutrient of the liver
    Basil
    Chamomile, Roman
    Clove
    Cypress
    Elemi
    Helichrysum
    Juniper
    Ledum
    Lemon
    Lemongrass
    Mountain Savory
    Myrtle
    Oregano
    Pepper, Black

Petitgrain
Rosemary
Spikenard
Spruce
Tansy, Idaho
Thyme, Linalol
Tsuga
Vetiver

Strength, nutrient of the stomach
Ginger
Lavender
Lemongrass
Myrrh
Orange
Spikenard
Tangerine

Teachable, nutrient of the Muscular System
Basil
Goldenrod
Helichrysum
Laurus Nobilis
Lavender
Ledum
Oregano
Rosewood
Sandalwood
Spruce
Spearmint
Tansy, Idaho
Wintergreen

Temperance, nutrient of the Digestive System
- Cedarwood
- Chamomile, Roman
- Dill
- Eucalyptus Globilus
- Fennel
- Fir (Abies alba)
- Lavender
- Lemongrass
- Myrtle
- Oregano
- Peppermint
- Spikenard
- Spearmint
- Tarragon
- Thyme, Linalol

Truth, nutrient of the Integumentary System
- Eucalyptus Polybrachtea
- Helichrysum

Unity, nutrient of the Immune System
- Bergamot
- Cistus
- Fennel
- Frankincense
- Goldenrod
- Jasmine
- Lavender
- Ledum
- Melaleuca Alternifolia
- Melaleuca Ericifolia

Patchouli
Pepper, Black
Petitgrain
Pine
Rosemary
Rosemary Verbenon
Rosewood
Spruce
Tansy, Idaho
Thyme

Uplifted, nutrient of the bladder
Grapefruit
Helichrysum
Laurus Nobilis
Ledum
Marjoram
Melaleuca Alternifolia
Melaleuca Ericifolia
Mountain Savory
Oregano
Patchouli
Pepper, Black
Petitgrain
Pine
Rosewood
Sage
Spearmint
Wintergreen

The Essential Oils by Positive States

"Science has demonstrated, for example, that specific feelings produce a predictable chemistry in our bodies that corresponds to that particular feeling. As we change our feelings, we change our chemistry. We literally have what may be viewed as 'hate chemistry,' 'anger chemistry,' 'love chemistry,' and so on. Biological expressions of emotion appear in our bodies as the levels of hormones, antibodies, and enzymes present in our state of wellness."
The Isaiah Effect, Gregg Braden

Accept truth	Laurus Nobilis
Acceptance	Nutmeg, Jasmine
Accepted	Clary Sage, Jasmine, Myrtle, Peppermint, Geranium, Grapefruit
Accept self	Thyme
Accepting	Tsuga
Acclaimed	Fennel
Acknowledged	Jasmine, Rosemary Verbenon
Accelerated	Ylang-Ylang

Adaptable	**Rosemary**
Admirable	**Galbanum, Goldenrod**
Affable	**Mountain Savory**
Agreeable	**Eucalyptus Globilus, Eucalyptus Polybrachtea**
Aligned	**Spikenard**
Appreciated	**Sandalwood**
Approval	**Basil**
Assertive	**Lemongrass**
Assured	**Dill**
Assurance	**Eucalyptus Polybrachtea**
Attended to	**Tansy**
Authentic	**Valerian**
Balanced	**Laurus Nobilis**
Bearable	**Basil**
Benevolence	**Peppermint**
Blissful	**Cistus**
Calm	**Ledum, Marjoram, Melaleuca Alternifolia**
Care, about self	**Sandalwood**
Care (taken care of)	**Valerian**
Careful	**Galbanum**
Caring	**Geranium, Ravensara**
Capable	**Vitex, Wintergreen**
Centered	**Pine**
Chaste	**Cypress**
Cheerful	**Melaleuca Alternifolia, Myrrh**
Cherished	**Galbanum, Lemongrass**
Comforted	**Cedarwood, Roman Chamomile**

THE ESSENTIAL OILS BY POSITIVE STATES

Comfortable	Black Pepper
Commended	Spearmint
Competent	Ginger
Comprehending	Vetiver
Concerned	Fir (Abies Alba)
Confident	Bergamot, Geranium
Connected	Rosewood
Considerate	Nutmeg, Thyme (Linalol)
Contentment	Myrtle
Cooperative	Wintergreen
Coordinated	Thyme, Linalol
Courageous	Marjoram
Decent	Dill
Decisive	Oregano
Delighted	Lavender
Determined	Rosemary
Dignified	Valerian
Directed	Tangerine
Disciplined	Rosemary Verbenon
Disguised	Tsuga
Efficient	Red Canadian Cedar
Embraces Truth	Melissa
Enough (I'm)	Tsuga
Enthused	Tangerine
Exceptional	Cinnamon Bark
Exuberant	Hyssop
Faith in Self and God	Geranium
Faithful	Ledum
Favored	Clary Sage

Feeling	Pine
Finished	Roman Chamomile
Flexible	Rosewood
Flowing	Ravensara
Focused	Rose
Forgiveness	Eucalyptus Polybrachtea, Fir (Abies Alba), Nutmeg, Thyme (Linalol)
Forgiveness, Total	Cistus, Lavender
Forgiveness, (Unconditional	Frankincense
Free of Burdens	Thyme
Fulfillment	Ravensara
Spiritual Minded	Frankincense, Ledum, Marjoram
Good	Goldenrod, Petitgrain
Good Luck	Melaleuca Ericifolia
Graceful	Cypress
Grateful	Cinnamon Bark
Happy	Helichrysum, Lavender
Healthy	Myrrh
Honest	Oregano
Honored	Marjoram
Humble	Petitgrain
Included	Basil, Sage
Indispensable	Tansy
Inspired	Pine
Invigorated	Coriander, Helichrysum, Tangerine
In Tune	Pine

THE ESSENTIAL OILS BY POSITIVE STATES

Joy	Ginger
Joy, Supreme	Mountain Savory, Rose
Joyful	Eucalyptus Radiate, Ginger
Kind	Cedarwood, Petitgrain
Liberated	Cypress, Tangerine
Life Works For Me	Cinnamon Bark
Looking Forward	Melaleuca Alternifolia, Peppermint
Love, Can Demonstrate	Hyssop
Love, Unconditional	Hyssop, Myrrh, Spearmint
Loveable	Valerian
Loved	Cistus
Loving	Eucalyptus Globilus, Helichrysum, Jasmine
Mellow	Oregano
Merciful	Ledum
Mindful	Grapefruit
Moving Forward	Tarragon
Motivated	Cedarwood, Cinnamon Bark, Vetiver
Nurtured	Mountain Savory
Open	Peppermint
Open-Minded	Vetiver
Pardoned	Fir (Abies Alba)

Passionate	Melaleuca Ericifolia
Peace	Eucalyptus Globilus, Geranium, Grapefruit, Laurus Nobilis, Nutmeg
Peaceful	Cedarwood, Fennel, Black Pepper, Ravensara
Peace Of Mind	Clove
Pleasant	Hyssop, Orange
Plenty of Room	Roman Chamomile
Powerful	Eucalyptus Radiate, Fennel, Sandalwood
Praised	Clove
Proficient	Spruce
Progressing	Vitex
Progressive	Ylang-Ylang
Prosperous	Grapefruit
Provided For	Geranium
Radiant	Tarragon
Reasonable	Tsuga
Refreshed	Thyme
Regarded Highly	Thyme
Relaxed	Orange
Released	Myrtle
Reliable	Melissa
Remembered	Ravensara
Renewed	Clary Sage, Sage
Responsible	Petitgrain
Resolute	Elemi
Respect	Fennel
Respectful	Lemon
Responsive	Coriander, Ginger

THE ESSENTIAL OILS BY POSITIVE STATES

Reverent	**Marjoram**
Safe	Fir (White)
Selfless	Red Canadian Cedar
Sensitive	Cistus
Serene	Helichrysum, Jasmine, Black Pepper
Sought After	Rose
Stable	Geranium, Goldenrod
Stability	Frankincense
Steadfast	Cypress, Elemi, Eucalyptus Radiate, Thyme
Strong	Clove, Ginger
Submissive	Basil
Supported	Clary Sage
Sure	Elemi
Teachable	Spruce
Tenacious	Juniper
Thoughtful	Peppermint
Tolerance	Galbanum
Tranquil	Jasmine
Trust	Coriander
Trustworthy	Grapefruit
Uplifted	Spikenard
Understanding	Grapefruit
Unrestrained	Goldenrod
Upright	Vetiver
Unselfish	Spearmint
Valiant	Lemon
Valued	Clove, Grapefruit

Vibrant	**Lavender**
Vindicated	**Black Pepper**
Virtuous	**Galbanum**
Welcomed	**Jasmine**
Winsome	**Jasmine**
Wise	**Bergamot, Spikenard**
Worthy	**Eucalyptus Globilus**
Yielding	**Spruce**

The Essential Oils vs. Negative States

"For instance, criticism indulged in long enough will often lead to dis-eases such as arthritis. Anger turns into things that boil and burn and infect the body. Resentment long held festers and eats away at the self and ultimately can lead to tumors and cancer. Guilt always seeks punishment and leads to pain." Heal Your Body, Louise L. Hay, Page 7

Accused	**Geranium**
Agitated	**Helichrysum**
Alienated	**Lemongrass**
Animosity	**Petitgrain**
Angry	**Pine**
Anguish	**Nutmeg**
Anxiety, Chronic	**Geranium**
Bad Luck	**Melaleuca Ericifolia**
Bashful	**Mountain Savory**
Banished	**Geranium, Grapefruit, Jasmine, Myrtle**
Beaten Down	**Hyssop**

Belligerent	**Melaleuca Alternifolia, Myrrh**
Betrayed	**Oregano**
Boiling Inside	**Ledum**
Boxed In	**Clary Sage, Helichrysum, Ravensara**
Bragging	**Lemon**
Careless	**Galbanum**
Clingy	**Lemongrass**
Closed Off	**Helichrysum**
Clumsy	**Cypress**
Competitive	**Fennel, Peppermint**
Compromised	**Marjoram**
Contrary	**Eucalyptus Globilus, Eucalyptus Polybrachtea**
Cowardice	**Basil, Red Canadian Cedar**
Defeated	**Juniper**
Degradation	**Red Canadian Cedar, Cypress, Galbanum**
Despised	**Galbanum**
Discord	**Lavender, Melaleuca Alternifolia**
Disheartened	**Marjoram**
Dirty	**Goldenrod**
Disapproval	**Frankincense, Jasmine**
Discredited	**Clary Sage, Eucalyptus Polybrachtea**
Distraught	**Ravensara**
Dreadful	**Myrrh**

THE ESSENTIAL OILS VS. NEGATIVE STATES

Driven	Hyssop, Marjoram, Orange
Drowning (Like I'm)	Nutmeg
Emotional Stress	Fir (Abies Alba)
Empty	Ravensara
Enraged	Petitgrain, Pine
Enslaved	Goldenrod, Mountain Savory, Black Pepper
Entangled	Myrtle
Fatigued	Clove
Fainthearted	Spearmint
Fearful	Lemon
Feeling Old	Rose
Feeling Poor	Pine
Fierce	Rose
Forlorn	Tansy
Friendless	Tangerine
Frightened	Coriander
Frigid	Hyssop, Melaleuca Ericifolia
Goofed	Eucalyptus Polybrachtea
Grief	Ginger, Black Pepper
Grieved	Ledum
Grudges	Hyssop
Harmony	Pine
Hateful	Eucalyptus Globulus
Hesitant	Lemongrass
Hopeless	Rosewood

Inconsistency	Frankincense
Ignored	Jasmine
Immobilized	Spikenard
Imposter	Grapefruit
Irked	Melaleuca Alternifolia
Insecure	Coriander, Dill
Insanity	Goldenrod
Intolerant	Galbanum, Helichrysum
Know-It-All	Bergamot
Livid	Myrrh
Longing	Geranium, Spikenard
Lost	Myrtle
Luckless	Rosemary, Spearmint
Lying	Rosewood
Martyr	Tansy
Melancholy	Roman Chamomile
Morbid	Black Pepper
Murmuring	Peppermint
Naïve	Tarragon
Needing Approval	Goldenrod
Needs Protection	Geranium
Neglected	Lemongrass
Nervous	Jasmine
Neurotic Attachments	Rose
Not Enough, I'm	Spearmint
Obnoxious	Mountain Savory
Obstinate	Tarragon

THE ESSENTIAL OILS VS. NEGATIVE STATES

Obsessed	Spruce
Overworked	Peppermint
Pettiness	Cinnamon Bark
Pigeon-Holed	Helichrysum
Punished	Cedarwood
Pushed	Orange
Quitting	Ginger, Patchouli
Repelling Others	Coriander, Tangerine
Repressed	Grapefruit, Laurus Nobilis
Reprobate	Ledum
Repulsed By Others	Hyssop
Resentment	Oregano
Restless	Melaleuca Ericifolia
Reticent	Melaleuca Alternifolia
Ridiculous	Rosemary Verbenon
Ruined	Clove
Rushed	Myrrh
Sad	Eucalyptus Radiate
Scum	Lemon
Self-Centered	Jasmine
Self-Condemnation	Nutmeg
Self-Conscious	Melaleuca Ericifolia
Self-Contempt	Sandalwood
Shameful	Goldenrod
Shocked	Clove, Petitgrain
Shunned	Ravensara
Shoved Aside	Helichrysum, Hyssop

Sinking	Tansy
Slothful	Spruce
Stagnant	Rosemary
Strife	Myrtle
Struggling	Cistus
Suicidal	Cinnamon Bark, Petitgrain
Suspicious	Fir (White)
Temptation	Patchouli
Tentative	Geranium
Thoughtless	Grapefruit
Ticked Off	Clary Sage
Timid	Basil, Mountain Savory, Sage
Touchy	Patchouli
Trapped	Cypress, Ravensara
Tribulation	Spikenard
Troubled	Cedarwood, Eucalyptus Globilus
Ugly	Black Pepper
Unappreciated	Coriander
Unbearable	Cedarwood
Uncomfortable	Lemongrass
Unfeeling	Fir (Abies Alba)
Unforgiveness	Eucalyptus Polybrachtea
Unhappy	Eucalyptus Globilus
Unjust	Laurus Nobilis
Unkind	Marjoram, Orange
Unloved	Galbanum, Jasmine, Spruce

Unmindful	Lemongrass
Unprepared	Bergamot
Unqualified	Ginger
Unresolved	Roman Chamomile
Upset	Helichrysum
Unsettled	Basil, Cypress, Dill, Elemi, Eucalyptus Radiate
Unsupported	Basil, Ledum
Unsure	Cinnamon Bark, Elemi, Eucalyptus Polybrachtea
Unworthy	Eucalyptus Globilus
Used	Sage
Useless	Lemon, Sandalwood
Vengeance	Juniper
Victim	Tarragon
Violated	Myrrh
Vulnerable	Cistus
Weak	Clove, Eucalyptus Radiata, Rosemary Verbenon
Weariness	Melaleuca Ericifolia, Rose

Summary

The Respiratory System's nutrient is Love.
Love cannot be defined by anything–it is everything.
- Kindness is the nutrient of the lungs.

The Cardiovascular System's nutrient is Joy.
Joy is unbridled happiness, a happiness that permeates every cell of our being.
- Meaning is the nutrient of the heart.
- Making progress is the nutrient of the blood.

The Endocrine System's nutrient is Peace.
Peace is an awareness that responds appropriately.
- Certainty is the nutrient of the thyroid.
- Sensibility is the nutrient of the adrenals.

The Excretory System's nutrient is Patience.
Patience is calm endurance and patient waiting.
- Uplifted is the nutrient of the bladder.

SUMMARY

The Nervous System's nutrient is Gentleness.
Gentleness is great strength combined with sensitivity.
- Justice is the nutrient of the brain.

The Skeletal System's nutrient is Quality.
Quality is that which makes us feel capable, fit, competent, and able to enjoy the goodness of life.

The Muscular System's nutrient is Teachable.
Being teachable is being open and ready for change.

The Digestive System's nutrient is Temperance.
Temperance is governed by the value we place on ourselves; this value gives us the ability to have proper self-restraint.
- Authenticity is the nutrient of the colon.
- Stability is the nutrient of the liver.
- Highly Valued is the nutrient of the small intestines.
- Strength is the nutrient of the stomach.

The Reproductive System's nutrient is Faith.
Faith is belief coupled with conviction and accomplished through experience.
- Consciousness is the nutrient of the uterus.
- Invigorated and productive are the nutrients of the prostate.
- Self-esteem is the nutrient of the testes.
- Optimism is the nutrient of the ovaries.

The Lymphatic System's nutrient is Forgiveness.
Forgiveness is the ability to stay connected to one's true self.
- Loyalty is the nutrient of the pancreas.
- Assurance is the nutrient of the kidneys.

The Integumentary System's nutrient is Truth.
Truth is resilient and stands the test of time. It is proven over and over.
- Reliability is the nutrient of the skin.

Unity is the nutrient of the Immune System.
Unity is an internal movement to create.

Client Testimonials

"I used Joy Cell on my hands and loved it because it worked within an hour to take the swelling out of my tongue and took away my sore throat from a wheat allergy reaction after eating a muffin." **-Tana, Great Falls, MT**

"We have been clients of Claudia Burdick for approximately 13 years. When my children were newborn and 3 ½ years old, I was referred to her by a friend who said, 'When you don't know what else you can do, you need to talk to Claudia!'

Our son's health has been an issue for us in various capacities his whole life. I honestly don't know where we would be today had we not met her and worked with her to get him to be where he is now.

My daughter suffered from allergies, chronic yeast infections, and intolerances to many things. She, too, has a greater enjoyment of life because of Claudia and her work.

We have often tested, tried, and given feedback on many different methods that Claudia has learned and developed as she has asked us to help her in her quest of healing and making people well. We have believed in her steadfast pursuit of learning for all of us to feel well and feel better in order to experience an improved state of health.

She doesn't stop until you are well and has worked relentlessly in pursuit of our best health. We are a healthier, happier family because of her hard work, products, and knowledge!" -**Melanie, Helena, MT**

"I had a lot of trouble sleeping when I was pregnant. I would sleep for 2 hours, then wake up and not be able to get back to sleep for 6 hours. When I started saying affirmations, I was able to sleep normally again. When I would forget to say my affirmations, or I needed new ones, I would start having problems sleeping again.

I also had pretty severe back pain while pregnant, which made it difficult for me to walk, even to go grocery shopping or normal activities. Saying my affirmations helped with this as well. At times I would forget to say them, wonder why I was having so much trouble walking, then realize I had forgotten to say my affirmations, say them consistently for a day, then be back to feeling pain-free.

It seems incredible that saying words could have such a physical affect, but for me it made a marked physical difference." -**Rebekah, Seattle, WA**

CLIENT TESTIMONIALS

"I am a real estate agent and spend a lot of time on the computer. I had been having carpal tunnel syndrome since my second pregnancy. It was something I thought I'd have to live with unless I wanted to undergo surgery. I began rubbing the oil tincture on my palms and was amazed that within a week the carpal tunnel pain, which I have been suffering with for 17 years, is completely gone. I haven't used any other product for the carpal tunnel and have been completely satisfied and amazed at the results!"
- **Susi, Seattle, WA**

"I had all of my colon removed except the descending colon due to colon cancer in 2005. I have had a lot of pain from my bowels cramping. The oil blends for the emotional field, such as shake hands-crocus and others have really been a Godsend. I use them several times a day and sometimes I apply them every 15 minutes if the pain is persistent. They always relieve the pain and I am so grateful. I wouldn't have much quality of life without them." -**Valerie, Seattle, WA**

"I have had the privilege of using most of these products for extended periods of time over the last few years. Each product has brought with it a variety of rewarding experiences. I am very sensitive to subtle energies, and with each new product worn I have felt a new wealth of energy being introduced into my life immediately. These products are my medicine of choice. I use them on myself, my children, and my pets.

I cannot say enough good things about them because they have enhanced my life so much. Each organ and each system in my body had been addressed and supported and I have found that I am beginning to embody love, joy, and peace in all of my daily dealings. These products have been helping me to transform into the whole and full me. I have found that with each new lesson that has come my way these products have been there to support me through the change. From fear to faith, from worthless to priceless.

    I lost 15 pounds using the products in the temperance chapter and had so many beautiful experiences in learning to value myself that I feel I could write a whole book about them. I have a set of the mandalas and intuitively choose which ones to wear each day. They not only offer the specific positive energy but also serve as a constant reminder to be Teachable, or to Trust. I wear my Faith Mandala when I need to trust myself in making a decision. I also wear it when speaking in public, flying on a plane or having my monthly cycle.

    I've had a powerful experience with the Forgiveness Mandala where it felt as though the messages came out of the mandala and systematically unlocked each area of my body that had been locked in un-forgiveness for not valuing myself. I was overwhelmed when it reached my lungs with a deep feeling of forgiveness for smoking for so many years. I am thankful to have these products to hold my hand on this journey of life." -**Shy, Helena, MT**

    "I often feel off-balanced. People have even thought that I have been drinking because I get dizzy and my vision gets distorted, like everything is super-imposed.

My speech goes and then I get very dehydrated. The triz boxes helped me feel more focused and start to clear my vision. When I start to really get off-balanced, the moieties really help. I've also had an on-going infection since birth and have tried everything to get rid of it. Nothing worked. The rescuers really worked for this issue and I have been infection free for 4 months." -**Wanda, Helena, MT**

Resources

Websites:

www.burdickinstitute.com	Health is in the Spirit website – For products listed on Products Quick Reference.
www.essencesonline.com	Findhorn Flower Essences & Bach Flower Essences
www.younglivingus.co	Essential Oils
www.desertalchemy.com	Desert Flower Essences
www.luminanti.com	Tuning Forks
www.alaskanessences.com	Alaskan Flower Essences & Gem Elixirs
www.thework.com	Byron Katie's work

Books:

The Body Magnetic by Buryl Payne, Ph.D., 6th Edition, 1996

Loving What Is, by Byron Katie

The Alchemy of the Desert by Cynthia Athina Kemp Scherer

RESOURCES

A Guide to the Alaskan Essences by Steve Johnson

Essential Desk Reference by Essential Science Publishing

Bach Flower Essence, Theory & Practice by Mechthild Scheffer

The Complete Book of Flower Essences by Rhonda Pallasdowney

Taber's Cyclopedic Medical Dictionary

Theory of Colors, Johann Von Goethe (1840)

There's A Spiritual Solution to Every Problem, Wayne W. Dyer

Cure Your Own Allergies in Minutes, Dr. Jimmy Scott, Ph.D.

List of Contributors and acknowledgements:

Thank you, Shy Mitchell, for all your encouragement and support along with providing the cover picture, quotes, and editing. Many long hours we spent together exploring. You've been a wonderful inspiration.

I would also like to thank Lonita Dalton for her untiring help with editing and encouragement.

Thank you, Lisa from www.poignantpen for your suggestions and help with editing.

A big thank you also goes to all of my family, friends, and clients for believing in me and the work that I am doing.

I especially want to thank my husband, Dan, for all the years he has supported me in my endeavors and search for truth, always with unconditional love.

LIST OF CONTRIBUTORS AND ACKNOWLEDGEMENTS:

Thank you to my sons, Dustin, Joe, Kip, James, and Paul who have always stood by me and believed in me. This has meant so much. Each one of you is a priceless gift that I thank God for everyday. You are the reasons that I have dared to go deep into the unknown looking for answers.

I would also like to thank my daughter-in-law Sunny who has come into the family and embraced all that we do and all of us with open arms and an open heart. She has helped me with ideas, designs, and packaging and with the creation of the products.

Endnotes

i   Terra Spun Device – The Terra Spun Device was created when there was a need to energize and amp up the frequencies contained in essential oils, flower essences, and herbal products. We found that by using this device we could in minutes accomplish what previously took much more time and effort. The Terra Spun contains a large natural quartz crystal, which is connected to an energy source. There is no need to recharge the energy source as the Terra Spun is a continuous loop of energy. These devices have been created in a very limited quantity, but are available from www.burdickinstitute.com. ©

ii

Made in the USA
Lexington, KY
15 August 2015